D. H. Lawrence
as Anti-Rationalist:

Mysticism, Animism and Cosmic Life in His Works

Takeo Iida

Published by

MELROSE BOOKS

An Imprint of Melrose Press Limited
St Thomas Place, Ely
Cambridgeshire
CB7 4GG, UK
www.melrosebooks.co.uk

FIRST EDITION

Copyright © Takeo Iida 2014

The Author asserts his moral right to
be identified as the author of this work

Cover designed by Jonathan Duval

ISBN   978-1-909757-16-5

Printed and bound in Great Britain by:
Grosvenor Group (Print Services) Ltd
London

CONTENTS

INTRODUCTION

The purpose of this book is to demonstrate D. H. Lawrence as a mystic and animistic writer and as a perceiver of cosmic life in his poetry, prose works and paintings. Lawrence's mysticism is sometimes referred to or discussed by Robert A. Durr, L. D. Clark, C. J. P. Lee and Akinobu Ohkuma but none of them consider Lawrence as a mystic in his meditative poems, which I think deserve more attention.

The first three chapters will consider Lawrence as a mystic poet, which seems most evident in 'The Ship of Death' (which describes the soul's journey into the darkness and its rebirth) and other meditative poems in *Last Poems* (or *The Last Poems Notebook* of the Cambridge edition of the *Poems*).

The following seven chapters will discuss Lawrence as an animistic writer, which can be observed in many of his poems, stories, essays and paintings. His animistic perception in his works is not only a literary device but is also based essentially on his own felt experience, just like his mystic experience in his meditative poems. Although some critics have paid attention to his animistic perception they do not place much value on his felt experience, as such, in a modern age which belittles it. His mystic and animistic experiences are antithetical to both modern materialism and rationalism, the dominance of which Lawrence severely criticizes in many of his works. In this respect he can be called an anti-rationalist who goes against the modern tendency. Yet he does not irrationally resort to either animalism or primitivism. He believes that too much rationalism kills our intuitive sense of life and what he insists on, therefore, is the restoration of the balance between reason and intuition. Being critical of the modern tendency, he incorporates mystic or animistic experience into his works so that modern readers may be awakened to either of those senses: they have too long forgotten or suppressed their own mystic or animistic sense of life under the dominant rules of rationalism and materialism.

In Europe there is 'a very old tradition' of anti-rationalism, as Constatine Nicholas Starvou indicates in his comparative study on William Blake and D. H. Lawrence: 'the Essenes, early Franciscans, mystics such as Swedenborg, philosophers such as Berkley and the "Romantics" – all may be said to belong to this tradition (vii).

Early Greek philosophers such as Heraclitus and Parmenides, whom he does not refer to here, were of course also called anti-rationalists in ancient Greece. When the young Lawrence studied these early Greek philosophers by reading John Burnet's *Early Greek Philosophy* he realized that the long-forgotten tradition of anti-rationalism was extremely significant in human life in modern times, especially in an age of rationalism and materialism (which he feared would suppress the intuitive sense of life on every level).

The modern age inevitably made Lawrence take an anti-rationalistic attitude, although he was also a very discursive thinker. This is evident in many essays, such as *Fantasia of the Unconscious*, *Studies in Classic American Literature*, *Study of Thomas Hardy*, *Education of the People* and *Apocalypse* or 'The Reality of Peace'. In a letter dated 1 April 1917 he confessed his own philosophical preference for 'pure abstract thought' (*L* iii 110).

His anti-rationalistic attitude should not be regarded as his own particular standpoint but should be considered historically within Europe's long anti-rationalism tradition. Thus, the first three chapters will consider Lawrence as a mystic in relation to early Greek philosophers, medieval and modern Christian mystics, metaphysical poets and other mystic writers in European history.

In Europe there is another (though obscure) tradition of animism, which can be observed in Europe's polytheistic Celtic, Germanic and Greco-Roman deities. It appears to have been long dead, yet Lawrence tries to revive its perceptions in his writing, for example, in *The White Peacock*, *St. Mawr*, 'The Last Laugh', 'Pan in America' and *Lady Chatterley's Lover*. In these works Lawrence tries to revitalize his readers' sense of life by bringing them back into a living connection with the spirit of earth; the Great Mother. This will be discussed in Chapters 4 to 10.

Lawrence's animistic perception reminds us of his closeness to Japanese writers. Chapters 9 to 10 will also therefore consider the universality of Lawrence's animistic worldview by comparing it with the animistic perception of Japanese writers, which is relatively similar to that of Lawrence.

The last two chapters will also refer to Japanese artistic achievements. Chapter 11 compares Lawrence's attitude toward sex with that of Japan's well-known Lawrentian novelist Sei Ito, whose novels describe sexual scenes like Lawrence's: this indicates both their similarity and essential difference.

Unlike the preceding chapters the last one, though dealing with such Japanese Ukiyoe painters as Hiroshige and Hokusai, is not a critical essay but a short note. Its aim is just to correct Lawrence's erroneous (though brief) comment on the turtle picture dust jacket of his poetry book *Tortoises* by comparing it with Hiroshige's Ukiyoe print *Fukagawa Mannen Bridge* and to rescue the latter from Lawrence's, and subsequent critics', misunderstanding of it. It is obvious that without seeing Hiroshige's print Lawrence thought his turtle dust jacket was 'a complete print': my research revealed that it was not 'a complete print' but an unknown illustrator's clever imitation of Hiroshige's original print.

All the chapters of this book are based on the papers which were originally published in journals or books. Some of them were slightly revised for the purpose of this book but the original content of each paper is kept intact as was published in the journals or books. Heinemann, Viking and Penguin editions of Lawrence's works were used for citation in many of the original papers but this time they are all replaced for consistency with the authoritative Cambridge edition of Lawrence's works, including the latest edition of the *Poems*. Since the Penguin edition of the *Complete Poems* includes unpublished juvenile poems, while the *Poems* does not, the former is sometimes referred to as *CP* when comparing a published poem with its earlier unpublished one (or just in reference).

ACKNOWLEDGEMENTS

Acknowledgements are due to the editors of the journals and books in which the following papers were originally published:

'On a Topos Called the Sun Shining at Midnight in D. H. Lawrence's Poetry', *The D.H. Lawrence Review* 15 (3) (1982);

'D. H. Lawrence's "The Ship of Death" and Other Poems in *Last Poems*', *Studies in English Literature* (Tokyo: Literary Society of Japan) 58 (1) (1981);

'D. H. Lawrence: the Bible and the Mystics', *Etudes Lawrenciennes* 35 (2007);

'Lawrence's Pagan Gods and Christianity', *The D.H. Lawrence Review* 23 (12–13) (1991);

'Nature Deities: Reawakening Blood Consciousness in the Europeans', *Etudes Lawrenciennes* 10 (1994);

'The World of Animism in Contrast with Christianity in *St. Mawr*', *The Journal of the D. H. Lawrence Society 1997* (UK);

'*St. Mawr*, *The Escaped Cock* and *Child of the Western Isles*: the Revival of an Animistic Worldview in the Modern World', *The Journal of the D. H. Lawrence Society 1999* ;

'Lawrence's Pan Worship and Green Man Image', *D. H. Lawrence Studies* (Korea) 12 (3) (2004);

'The Universality of D.H. Lawrence's Animistic Vision', *D.H. Lawrence and Literary Genre*, ed. Simonetta de Filippis and Nick Ceramella (Napoli: Loffredo Editore, 2004);

'D. H.Lawrence and Akiko Yosano: Contemporary Poets of Human Touch and Cosmic Life', *D. H. Lawrence:Literature, History, Culture,* ed. Keith Cushman, Michael Bell, Takeo Iida and Hiro Tateishi (Tokyo: Kokusho Kankoukai Press, 2005);

'D. H. Lawrence and Sei Ito: Characteristics of the Sexual Scenes in Their Novels', *Comparative Cultural Studies of Kurume University* 25 (2000);

'A Response to Keith Cushman's "Lawrence's Dust-Jackets: Addenda and Corrigendum"', *DHLR* 31 (3) (2003) (these 12 papers are arranged in this order for each chapter).

Acknowledgements are also due to: Lawrence Pollinger Ltd., the literary executor of D.H. Lawrence's estate, which is the copyright holder of Lawrence's works; Clive Hicks, whose photographs of the Green Man image are used in chapter 8; Shuei-sha Press, from whose publication (*Ukiyoe Taikei (Series)*) two Ukiyoe prints (Hiroshige's and Hokusai's) are photocopied and used in chapter 12.

I am also very grateful to many Lawrentian friends who supported me, especially those who often gave me useful advice or encouragement for my research: Peter Preston, Keith Cushman, Keith Sagar, Jack Stewart, Mara Kalnins, Jungmai Kim, Ginette Katz Roy, Anja Viinikka, Saburo Kuramochi, Shunji Suzuki and Hiro Tateishi. My thanks also go to my family: Masami, Shino and Sato and my long-time friend Stephen Grey – who helped me and my family wholeheartedly (with his family's cooperation) – while we stayed in England for the first time more than 30 years ago.

I would also like to dedicate this book to the distinguished Lawrentian Peter Preston, who helped me in many ways and on various occasions to continue my research (and who, regrettably, passed away in 2011).

Takeo Iida
Kurume, June, 2013.

A list of abbreviations of D. H. Lawrence's works used in this book:

A: *Apocalypse and the Writings on Revelation*, ed. Mara Kalnins. Cambridge: Cambridge University Press, 1979.

CP: *The Complete Poems of D. H. Lawrence,* ed. Vivian de Sola Pinto and Warren Roberts. Harmondsworth: Penguin, 1977.

EC: 'The Escaped Cock'. *The Virgin and the Gipsy and Other Stories,* ed. Michael Herbert, Bethan Jones and Lindeth Vasey. Cambridge: Cambridge University Press, 2005.

FCDL: *The Fox, The Captain's Doll, The Ladybird,* ed. Dieter Mehl. Cambridge: Cambridge University Press, 1992.

FU: 'Fantasia of the Unconscious'. *Psychoanalysis and the Unconscious and Fantasia of the Unconscious,* ed. Bruce Steele. Cambridge: Cambridge University Press, 2004.

FSLC: *The First and Second Lady Chatterley Novels,* ed. Dieter Mehl and Christa Jansohn. Cambridge: Cambridge University Press. 1999.

IR: *Introductions and Reviews,* ed. Neil Reeve and John Worthen. Cambridge: Cambridge University Press, 2005.

K: *Kangaroo,* ed. Bruce Steele. Cambridge: Cambridge University Press, 1994.

L i: *The Letters of D. H. Lawrence.* Vol. I: September 1901–May 1913, ed. James T. Boulton. Cambridge: Cambridge University Press, 1979.

L ii *The Letters of D.H. Lawrence.* Vol. II: June 1913–October 1916, ed. George J. Zytaruk and James T. Boulton. Cambridge: Cambridge University Press, 1981.

L iii: *The Letters of D.H. Lawrence.* Vol. III: October 1916–June 1921, ed. James T. Boulton and Andrew Robertson. Cambridge: Cambridge University Press, 1984.

L iv: *The Letters of D.H. Lawrence.* Vol. IV: June 1921–March 1924, ed. James T. Boulton, Elizabeth Mansfield and Warren Roberts. Cambridge: Cambridge University Press, 1987.

L v: *The Letters of D.H. Lawrence.* Vol. V: March 1924–March 1927, ed. James T. Boulton and Lindeth Vasey. Cambridge: Cambridge University Press, 1989.

LEA: *Late Essays and Articles,* ed. James T. Boulton. Cambridge: Cambridge University Press, 2004.

TAKEO IIDA

LCL: *Lady Chatterley's Lover. A Propos of Lady Chatterley's Lover,* ed. Michael Squires. Cambridge: Cambridge University Press, 1993.

MM: *Mornings in Mexico and Other Essays,* ed. Virginia Crosswhite Hyde. Cambridge: Cambridge University Press, 2009.

P: *The Plays,* ed. Hans-Wilhelm Schwarze and John Worthen. Cambridge: Cambridge University Press, 1999.

Poems: *The Poems of D.H. Lawrence*. Two vols., ed. Christopher Pollnitz. Cambridge: Cambridge University Press, 2013.

PS: *The Plumed Serpent,* ed. L.D. Clark. Cambridge: Cambridge University Press, 1987.

RDP: *Reflections on the Death of a Porcupine and Other Essays,* ed. Michael Herbert. Cambridge: Cambridge University Press, 1988.

SCAL: *Studies in Classic American Literature,* ed. Ezra Greenspan, Lindeth Vasey and John Worthen. Cambridge: Cambridge University Press, 2003.

StM: *St. Mawr and Other Stories,* ed. Brian Finney. Cambridge: Cambridge University Press, 1983.

TI: *Twilight in Italy and Other Essays,* ed. Paul Eggert. Cambridge: Cambridge University Press, 1994.

WL: *Women in Love,* ed. David Farmer, Lindeth Vasey and John Worthen. Cambridge: Cambridge University Press, 1987.

WP: *The White Peacock,* ed. Andrew Robertson. Cambridge: Cambridge University Press, 1983.

WWRA: *The Woman Who Rode Away and Other Stories,* ed. Dieter Mehl and Christa Jansohn. Cambridge: Cambridge University Press, 1995.

XIII

CHAPTER 1

ON A TOPOS CALLED THE SUN SHINING AT MIDNIGHT IN D.H. LAWRENCE'S POETRY

i

In his essay entitled 'Die Sonne leuchtet um Mitternacht: ein literarischer und religionsgeschichtlicher Topos in Ost und West' Professor Thomas Immoos discusses 'the sun shining at midnight' as a universal topos of eternal life (or light) in the mystery of darkness by giving various examples of it from Buddhist writings in the east and from Christian literature in the west. He says that the topos is a symbol of that eternal life in dark mystery which is actually felt only after you die to the old self completely (Immoos 482–500; 22–40).

His discussion reminds us of Lawrence's image of 'the dark sun' in *The Ladybird* (whose setting is in Europe) or *The Plumed Serpent* (whose setting is in the Mexican Indian community).[1] Although Professor Immoos does not mention Lawrence in the essay I think that the image of 'the dark sun' is also an example of the topos which is discussed in it and that the image is not only of Mexican Indian mythology (as it is elaborated in L. D. Clark's *Dark Night of the Body: D.H. Lawrence's* The Plumed Serpent (103–5)). I consider that it is also of European cultural tradition, i.e. Rosicrucian or alchemical thought (as *The Ladybird* suggests), Christian hymn tradition, Christian mysticism, ancient Greek philosophy, modern German philosophy and, finally, 17th century English metaphysical poetry. I will exemplify this thesis below.

ii

Lawrence uses the word 'darkness' or 'the dark' as possessing two meanings. One meaning of 'darkness' is the sense of sin, and this usage is traditionally Christian. The other points to ultimate mystery in cosmic life. The present discussion entails the second meaning.

'Midnight' in the topos of 'the sun shining at midnight' is an example of what Lawrence calls 'darkness' in the second meaning because 'midnight' in the topos implies ultimate mystery, while 'the sun' in the topos symbolizes eternal life glowing in ultimate mystery.

While the first appearance of the topos in Lawrence's prose seems to me to be the phrase 'the sun is dark' in *The Ladybird* (1923) the appearance of the nearest images to this topos in his poetry is in *Pansies* (1929), in which he uses the images of 'the sun of suns' and 'the immense sun behind the sun'. (See also 'the Hidden Sun' in the play *David* (1926), 'the dark sun' in *The Plumed Serpent* 1926) and 'the nameless Sun' in *Mornings in Mexico* (1927)).

But I think also that an embryonic stage of the topos can be seen in early poems (those poems written before *Look! We Have Come Through!* (1917)). The earliest poems are in the appendix of 'Juvenilia' in *The Complete Poems of D.H. Lawrence* (Penguin) (853–93).

In *Love Poems and Others* (1913) there is a poem entitled 'Red Moon-Rise', in which the following lines appear:

> For now I know
> That the Womb is a great red passion whence rises all
> The shapeliness that decks us here-below:
> Yea like the fire that boils within this ball
>
> Of earth, and quickens all herself with flowers,
> God burns within the stiffened clay of us (...) (*Love Poems* xxvii)

In this poem Lawrence uses the words 'the darkness' ('out of the twofold darkness') (xxvi) and 'the dark' ('I see the same red spark / As rose tonight upon us from the dark') (xxvii): the capitalized 'Womb' is a symbol for the ultimate darkness which produces every living thing. The Womb is not only darkness but also 'a great red passion' or 'the innermost fire' (xxvii).

(Years later he substituted 'the world within worlds' or 'the womb of the worlds' for 'the Womb' and introduced a new image, 'womb-fire' (*Poems* 55)). Although 'the innermost fire' is not exactly equivalent to 'the sun shining at midnight' it might be called fire 'at midnight': that is, fire in ultimate darkness.

In 'The Mystic Blue' (*Amores* (1916)) Lawrence writes:

> Out of the darkness, fretted sometimes in its sleeping,
> Jets of sparks in fountains of blue come leaping
> To sight, revealing a secret, numberless secrets keeping.
> (*Amores* 137 (see also its later version: 'Blueness', *Poems* 97))

The 'darkness' in the above extract is called 'Darkness abundant' in the last stanza of the poem:

> All these pure things come foam and spray of the sea
> Of Darkness abundant, which shaken mysteriously
> Breaks into dazzle of living, as dolphins leap from the sea
> Of midnight and shake it to fire, till the flame of the shadow we see.
> (*Amores* 138 (*Poems* 98))

Why is the 'Darkness' abundant? Because it seems that there is the fire of life in abundance in it. And out of the darkness come 'Jets of sparks in fountains of blue'. As the title of this poem suggests, an image of 'blue' is prominent in it. It is used in every stanza. Blue is a colour of life-glow and, therefore, the poem suggests that there is potential life-glow in blueness in 'Darkness abundant'.

There is another early poem of blue entitled 'Blue' in *Amores* in which there run the following lines:

> And I know the Host, the minute sparkling of darkness
> Which vibrates untouched and perfect through the grandeur of
> night,
> But which, when dawn crows challenge, assaulting the vivid motes
> Of living darkness, bursts fretfully, and is bright (…)
> (*Amores* 120 (see also its earlier version: 'What Do I Care?' *CP* 772))

The 'sparkling of darkness' comes out of darkness into the world of light when it dawns, but until then it lies in potentiality in darkness.

The image of fire or light in ultimate darkness (which is seen in these early poems) is also seen even in his 'Juvenilia', in which there is a fragmentary poem on sleep. In it Lawrence says:

> Ah life, God, Law, whatever name you have
> You great Will patient (struggling), you the sleep
> That does inform this various dream of living
> You stretched out forever, in whose body we
> Are bidden up as dreams, you great grand sleep
> Coursed round by rhythmic movement of the stars
> The constellations with your great heart the sun (…) (*CP* 869)

This shows that the heart of God is compared to the sun and that God dwells in the darkness of mystery, which is evidently shown by the following lines:

> And oh vast sleeper, still I am glad, for out
> Of thee there comes such new, such rarer
> Beauty of blowing dreams
> Oh Sleep, how art thou enriched
> Since I have seen, as never were seen before
> The men who are this body lapped
> In with thy darkness, move so subtle soft
> And gentle (...) (*CP* 871)

Since 'thy darkness' obviously means the darkness of God we can say that Lawrence uses 'darkness' in the sense of ultimate mystery, and 'the sun' as a symbol of the heart (or the burning flame of God) in this earliest poem.

However, there is no topos of 'the sun shining at midnight' in these early poems, though they have its variants. It is the same with *Look! We Have Come Through!* (1917) and *Birds, Beasts and Flowers* (1923).

Yet *Look!* distinguishes itself from the early poems which we have seen. It is in *Look!* that Lawrence sinks himself deep down in ultimate mystery – that is, he dies to the self and then his soul is newly created, being filled with life-fire in ultimate darkness. In the period of the early poems his ego persists, not coming to its total negation, though he feels ultimate darkness. He looks at the darkness – as it were – from outside, without plunging himself into it. He dare not do that because, as he recollects in 'New Heaven and Earth', he is ego-bound: 'everything was tainted with myself'. Therefore he could not let go of his ego.

In *Look!,* however, he throws himself into the midst of the unknown darkness in which the negation of himself is complete:

> God, but it is good to have died and been trodden out,
> trodden to nought in sour, dead earth,
> quite to nought
> absolutely to nothing (...) ('New Heaven and Earth', *Poems* 212)

This is the death of his ego. And then his soul is steeped in life-glow in the darkness because he continues:

> Green streams that flow from the innermost continent of the new
>   world,
> what are they?
> Green and illumined and travelling for ever
> dissolved with the mystery of the innermost heart of the continent,
> mystery beyond knowledge or endurance so sumptuous
> out of the well-heads of the new world. (*Poems* 214)

'Green streams' symbolizes life sparkle in the ultimate darkness, which is called 'the unknown' or 'the sources of mystery' in this poem.

Not only *Look!* but also *Birds* deals with the theme of the death of the old self and the succeeding renewal of it in darkness. Let us look at 'Medlars and Sorb-apples', for example:

> Going down the strange lanes of hell, more and more intensely
>   alone,
> The fibres of the heart parting one after the other
> And yet the soul continuing, naked-footed, ever more vividly
>   embodied

Like a flame blown whiter and whiter
In a deeper and deeper darkness
Ever more exquisite, distilled in separation. (*Poems* 236)

'A deeper and deeper darkness' implies that the soul plunges itself further and further down into darkness, and 'whiter and whiter' that it shines more brightly in a deeper darkness which pours life-flame into it. Here again is an image of glowing life in darkness. The image is also used in 'Snake', in which the snake is described as 'one of the lords / Of life' living in 'the underworld', which is a world of darkness. The lord of life is an image of life-flame which is, in the poem, in darkness (*Poems* 305).

Thus, the image of life-flame burning in darkness is seen in his 'Juvenilia', in *Love Poems and Others*, in *Amores*, in *Look!* and in *Birds*. After *Birds* comes *Pansies*, in which Lawrence makes new use of the image nearest to the topos of the sun shining at midnight: 'the sun of suns' or 'the immense sun behind the sun'.

In 'Underneath':

The earth leans its weight on the sun, and the sun on the sun of suns
Back and forth goes the balance and the electric breath.

The soul of man also leans in the unconscious inclination we call
   religion
towards the sun of suns, and back and forth goes the breath
of incipient energetic life. (*Poems* 416)

'What the old people call immediate contact with God' or 'communion with the godhead' is also called 'contact with the sun of suns' ('The Primal Passions', *Poems* 417). A similar expression to 'the sun of suns' is 'the immense sun behind the sun' ('Sun in Me', *Poems* 446). 'The sun of suns', which is a symbol of eternal life, is not to be seen with the eye because it is hidden as if behind the cloud of dark mystery.

The image of darkness is not expressed in 'the sun of suns' or 'the immense sun behind the sun' but implied in these poems, while it is explicitly expressed in one of the poems in *The Plumed Serpent* in which Lawrence uses an image of cave or 'Dark Eye':

In the cave which is called Dark Eye,
Behind the sun, looking through him as a window
Is the place. There the waters rise,
There the winds are born. (*PS* 114)

In the cave there sleeps Quetzalcoatl or, to use the image above, there dwells 'the sun of suns'. And in the novel Lawrence uses another image of 'the dark sun', which might be paraphrased as 'the sun of suns' in the mystery of darkness. The same can be said of the expression 'the sun is dark' in *The Ladybird*. Therefore, it might be said that 'the dark sun' is almost the same topos as 'the sun shining at midnight'.

Lawrence was instinctively aware, even from the earliest period, that there is life-flame in ultimate darkness. The awareness is quickened year by year and is reflected in each poetical work. While he uses the image of life-flame in darkness in his 'Juvenilia', in *Love Poems and Others*, in *Amores*, in *Look!* and in *Birds* he creates the most paradoxical image of 'the dark sun' in *The Ladybird* (1923) and *The Plumed Serpent* (1926). This image also occurs – along with its variants 'the Hidden Sun' or 'the sun of suns' in the play *David* (1926) (*P* 440, 518), 'the nameless Sun' in *Mornings in Mexico* (1927) (*MM* 84) (in which he also uses the image of 'the dark sun' at the centre of the earth) and 'the sun of suns' or 'the immense sun behind the sun' in *Pansies* (1929). The newly created image of 'the dark sun' is, of course, of Lawrence's origin: it has not only come out of his own pen but is deeply rooted in the soil of the tradition of the image, whether he was conscious of it or not. I will discuss this point below (section iii).

After *Pansies* and *Nettles* come *More Pansies* and *Last Poems* (1932) – which are included in the *CP* – or *The 'Nettles' Notebook* and *The Last Poems Notebook* in *Poems* (which do not exactly correspond to *More Pansies* and *Last Poems*). At any rate they do not have the image of 'the sun of suns' or 'the dark sun', yet they have similar images.

In 'God is Born', in *The 'Nettles' Notebook* (or *More Pansies*), Lawrence says:

Behold, God is born!
He is bright light!
He is pitch dark and cold! (*Poems* 589)

God is, therefore, of two sides. And in 'Bavarian Gentians', in *The Last Poems Notebook* (or *Last Poems*), Lawrence again uses the tone of 'a deeper and deeper darkness' which he had used in 'Medlars and Sorb-apples':

> Reach me a gentian, give me a torch!
> let me guide myself with the blue, forked torch of this flower
> down the darker and darker stairs, where blue is darkened on
>   blueness (...) (*Poems* 611)

Dis (or Pluto) is burning dark blue, not simply dark, in the underworld. So are the gentians. They are of 'the blue-smoking darkness, Pluto's dark blue daze, / black lamps from the halls of Dis, burning dark blue (...)' (*Poems* 610). Here, as in 'Blue' and 'The Mystic Blue', blue is an image of life-flame (which is in the darkness).

There is another interesting poem in *The Last Poems Notebook*: 'The Ship of Death'. Though it does not show us the dark sun image, it seems to suggest it behind the lines. After the ship of death – that is, 'the departing soul' – has sunken in dark oblivion in which 'darkness' is 'at one with darkness, up and down / and sideways utterly dark', 'out of eternity' there comes to 'the frail soul' 'a flush of yellow' or 'a flush of rose' (sections VII to X) (*Poems* 631–33).

The colours of yellow and red are those of life-glow and the ultimate source of the light might be surmised not as the physical sun at all but as 'the sun of suns' in darkness – in other words 'the dark sun' (I'll discuss 'The Ship of Death' in detail in the next chapter).

iii

In his essay 'New Mexico' Lawrence said that the experience of cosmic religion in New Mexico had almost 'shattered' his Christian background (*MM* 176), and he created the image of 'the dark sun' there. Obviously, Lawrence relied on Mexican mythology as one source in creating this image in the Mexican setting. But since the topos is a universal one, as Professor Immoos exemplifies in the above-mentioned essay, the origin of Lawrence's image seems to be not only in the Mexican mythological framework – as elaborated in Clark's *Dark Night of the Body* – but also in the European cultural framework, because the latter is more fundamental for Lawrence's spiritual growth even if he is severely critical of the spirit of the west. I maintain that his poetic insight was more strongly – even if unconsciously – influenced by European tradition (in the present case) by the topos which is traditionally seen in Europe, rather than by a new encounter with Mexican mythology and rituals performed in New Mexico. In fact, well before *The Plumed Serpent*, Lawrence had created 'the dark sun' image in *The Ladybird*.

In 1923 – three years before *The Plumed Serpent* – Lawrence wrote about 'the real original fire' through the mouth of Count Dionys, a Bohemian, in *The Ladybird*: 'The sun is dark' (*FCDL* 180). This is the same image as that in *The Plumed Serpent*. And Dionys and his family are, he says, initiated into the secrets and rites of 'a certain old secret society' 'like the freemasons' (*FCDL* 179): he is a European, and his 'dark sun' is certainly within the cultural framework of Europe. In the novel there is no statement of which society he belongs to, yet at least two possibilities of its identification could be pointed out.

First, his society – which he says was 'old' – will be such an old one as the Rosicrucian society whose brotherhood (known from the 16th century) is 'old' (Shapard, *Encyclopedia* II 787). In 1917 Lawrence read H. P. Blavatsky's *The Secret Doctrine* (and, in 1919, *Isis Unveiled*) (Burwell 251–52). She says in *The Secret Doctrine* that, 'according to the Rosicrucian tenets (…) light and darkness are identical in themselves, being only divisible in the human mind' (70). The words 'light and darkness are identical in themselves' could be said to be another expression of 'the sun is dark' or 'the dark sun'. (And far back in European history, according to Burwell, the Chaldeans had had a similar belief that 'the one universal light, which to man is darkness, is ever existent') (*The Secret Doctrine* 377).

A second possibility is that Count Dionys's society, though we do not know its name, seems to have a philosophy similar to that of an alchemical one, because the image nearest to 'the dark sun' in Europe is 'the sol niger' – that is, 'the black sun in alchemy'. This is cited in C. G. Jung's *Psychology and Alchemy,* which also cites 'dark light' on the same page (110). Jung says that both of these images symbolize the Monogenes, 'the Son of God' (107) in alchemists' writings. The 'sol niger' is, of course, mentioned in Professor Immoos's essay. Lawrence could not read this book, which was published in 1944 (14 years after his death). However, in 1918 he read another work by Jung – which may have been *On the Psychology of the Unconscious* (1917) (Burwell 248). In it there are some hints of 'sol niger' – for example, the 'night sea journey', Heraclitus's 'ever-living fire' and 'the sun' which saints behold in their visions (Jung, *On the Psychology* 68, 69, 99). It is possible that they contributed to Lawrence's formation of 'the dark sun' image, whether in *The Ladybird* or in *The Plumed Serpent*, if he did not know of the 'sol niger'.

The topos or its variant is also seen in the tradition of hymns. The nearest figure – in the historical sense – to Lawrence is a 19th-century hymn writer, John Keble, who writes that the throne of God is darkness in which there burns His flame:

> When God of old came down from heaven,
> In power and wrath He came;
> Before his feet the clouds were riven,
> Half darkness and half flame. (*Congregational Church Hymnal* No. 201)[2]

And one century before Keble, John Wesley writes in a similar vein:

> O Love! Thou bottomless abyss!
> My sins are swallowed up in Thee:
> Covered is my unrighteousness,
> Nor spot of guilt remains on me (...)
> With faith I plunge me in this sea;
> Here is my hope, my joy, my rest (...) (*Congregational Church Hymnal* no. 286)

The 'abyss' or the 'sea' suggests darkness and light suggests 'hope' or 'joy'. And the images are not – of course – of Wesley's own innovation, for they find their roots in the long tradition of Christianity. His brother, Charles Wesley, also writes:

> All praise to Him who dwells in bliss,
> Who made both day and night,

Whose throne is darkness in the abyss
Of uncreated light. (*The Methodist Hymn Book* no. 928)

The three hymns[3] immediately take us to the Bible, in which there are many examples of the image of God in darkness. I quote only three passages here:

And the people stood afar off and Moses drew near unto the
thick darkness where God was. (Exodus 20:21)

And ye came near and stood under the mountain; and the
mountain burned with fire unto the midst of heaven, with
darkness, clouds and thick darkness. And the Lord spake
unto you out of the midst of the fire. (Deuteronomy 4:11–12)

He made darkness his secret place; his pavilion round about
him were dark waters and thick clouds of the skies. (Psalms
18:11)

(I mention this in passing: an echo of 'dark waters' will be heard in the expression 'There the waters rise' in the poem in *The Plumed Serpent,* which we have already seen).

It is the Catholic mystics, prior to Protestants like John Keble and John and Charles Wesley, who inherited the image. Lawrence says, in *Mornings in Mexico*, that Europeans do not have any experience of concentrated meditation (58). He is right as far as he refers to his contemporaries. But when his argument is put in a European historical perspective it is off the point, because there is a long tradition of meditation with inner concentration – that is, the tradition of the Catholic mystics. There is, for example, St. Gregory of Nyssa from the 4th century, who describes the mystery of God as 'luminous darkness', according to G. A. Maloney's *Inward Stillness* (37). In the 5th century, Dionysius the Areopagite calls this mystery 'the dazzling obscurity' or 'the ray of the divine darkness' in *The Mystical Theology* (191, 192). And it is called 'the cloud of unknowing' in *The Cloud of Unknowing* by the anonymous 14th-century English mystic who says, 'reconcile yourself to wait in this darkness as long as is necessary (...) for if you are to feel him or to see him in this life it must always be in this cloud, in this darkness' (54). And when you are in this darkness, your soul will be pierced through by 'overwhelming spiritual light' (*The Cloud* 135). Paraphrasing 'the dark sun', we have called it the sun in the dark. This is quite parallel to the 'overwhelming spiritual light' in the 'darkness' in *The Cloud of Unknowing*.

Two centuries later St. John of the Cross says in *Dark Night of the Soul* that 'when the faculties had been perfectly annihilated and calmed, together with the passions, desires, and affections of the soul' (Peers I: 380), the eye of his soul saw the burning flame of God:

> In the happy night,
> In secret, when none saw me,
> Nor I beheld aught,
> Without light or guide, save that which burned in my heart.
> (Peers I: 325)[4]

'That which burned in my heart' is, of course, to borrow another expression of his 'living flame of love' (Peers III: 16). It burns in his heart in the intimate communication of union with the love of God. He says in the image of the sun in *Living Flame of Love*: 'When (...) the soul voids itself of all things and achieves emptiness and surrender of them' – that is, when the soul is in 'the happy night' –

> (...) it is impossible, if the soul does as much as in it lies, that
> God should fail to perform His own part by communicating
> Himself to the soul, at least secretly and in silence. It is more
> impossible than that the sun should fail to shine in a serene
> and unclouded sky. (Peers III: 167)

Perhaps Lawrence did not realize his own nearness to these mystics. However, his unconscious seems to have been rooted in the soil of the mystic tradition of the west because – as the examples above show – both the topos of the sun shining at midnight and its variations exist in western mystic tradition, which it seems was alive in his unconscious. Even if he had not known the Catholic mystics the topos or its variations could have been in his mind especially through the Bible, which he loved to read: the scriptures were, as he said, his 'flesh and blood' (*L* i 244) (de Sola Pinto 10; Kalnins 16).

Here we also have to consider another spiritual stratum of European tradition – that is, ancient Greek philosophy. It is well known that Lawrence read John Burnet's *Early Greek Philosophy* and Gilbert Murray's *Four Stages of Greek Religion* in 1916 (and its expanded edition, *Five Stages of Greek Religion*, in 1929) (Burwell 240, 242; Kalnins 13).[5]

Burnet says that 'the idea of the world breathing belonged to the earliest form of Pythagorianism, and there can be no difficulty in identifying this "boundless breath" with darkness, which stands very well for the unlimited.' And for Parmenides, too, darkness is considered to be the unlimited source (Burnet 186–87). This view of darkness is close to Lawrence's. In his discussion of ancient Greek mysticism, Professor Toshihiko Izutsu gives us a more illuminating interpretation than Burnet's: 'when you go down into utter darkness within you are in oneness with it', according to Parmenides and Xenophanes. 'Then out of the darkness there issues eternal light which illuminates the whole universe' (Izutsu 44: my translation). The mystic experience of ultimate reality was also shared by Heraclitus (Izutsu 45; Clark 105; Kalnins 13). There may be an echo of this light in darkness in sections VII to X in 'The Ship of Death' if the poem is interpreted as one which describes the soul's journey through darkness to eternal light.

In *Five Stages of Greek Religion*, Murray refers to Apuleius: 'he was initiated to Isis' and finally 'the sun shone upon him at midnight' (182). His experience is described in *The Golden Ass* as follows:

> I approached the very gates of death and set foot on Proserpine's threshold, yet was permitted to return, rapt through all the elements. At midnight I saw the sun shining as if it were noon; I entered the presence of the gods of the underworld and the gods of the upper-world, stood near and worshipped them. (241)

In fact, Apuleius both sank into utter darkness and saw the sun in this midnight darkness. Professor Immoos – in his essay – gives as an example the topos from this passage, and we might say that Apuleius's midnight sun is very similar to Lawrence's 'dark sun'. This seems natural, because the man 'of ancient Greek stock' and the modern English poet probably had a similar experience of sinking into darkness within and intuiting the sun or life-flame in it. The same will be said of those Christian and ancient Greek mystics whom we have seen above.

In the history of English literature, Lawrence had his predecessors in the use of the topos: Henry Vaughan, Thomas Traherne and George Herbert (Ichikawa 48; Smith 112–13).

It is not known whether Lawrence really read these poets or how much he studied their works. But it seems quite possible that he read and studied them considerably in his grammar school and college days. Professor James T. Boulton says this about Lawrence's education at Nottingham High School, an independent day school of ancient foundation, where he spent the years from 1898 to 1901:

> The influence it exerted on his intellectual growth has been curiously underestimated. He may have felt an outsider at the school; (…) but the quality of the education he received cannot be disregarded. He was taught by able graduate-teachers under Dr. James Gow (who became headmaster of Westminster School in London at the same time as Lawrence left the high school); he studied a broad curriculum, (…) including Natural Sciences as well as English language and literature, History, French and German. Interestingly, the emphasis in English and history was predominantly on the 17th century; this was also to be his chosen area of specialization in those subjects at University College, Nottingham. ('Introduction', *L* i 4)

Then, not underestimating Lawrence's reading experience of seventeenth century English literature, let us look at three examples of metaphysical poetry. In 'The Night', Vaughan says of 'Wise Nicodemus':

> Most blest believer he!
> Who in that land of darkness and blinde eyes
> Thy long expected healing wings could see,

When thou didst rise,
And what can never more be done,
Did at midnight speak with the Sun! (*Henry Vaughan* 358)

This poem is one of his aspiration for 'that night' 'where I in him / Might
live invisible and dim'. But 'The World' is a poem of his own experience
of 'that night' because he says:

I saw Eternity the other night
Like a great Ring of pure and endless light (…) (*Henry Vaughan*
299)

Traherne's 'Fullnesse' also expresses a similar experience:

A little Spark,
That shining in the Dark,
Makes, and encourages my Soul to rise. (*Thomas Traherne* 32)

In 'Even-Song', Herbert says in the Christian mystics' tone:

But thou art light & darknes both togeather:
If that bee dark we can not see,
The sunn is darker then a Tree,
And thou more dark then either.

Yet thou art not so dark, since I know this,
But that my darkness may touch thine,
And hope, that may teach it to shine,
Since Light thy Darknes is. (*George Herbert* 203)

Therefore, it might be said that the topos seen in the metaphysical poets
is nearly the same as Lawrence's: through the topos Lawrence is very
close to these Christian poets, even if he was not aware of the semblance.
It has been pointed out that Lawrence's poetry is like Wordsworth's (de
Sola Pinto 12; Marshall 107–08; Gilbert 12, 43) or like Blake's (Starvou
323–27; Marshall 106; Gilbert 55, 174, 219). I quite agree with this theory.

In addition, I maintain that Lawrence is like the metaphysical poets, too, as far as this topos is concerned.

The metaphysical poets' topos also reminds us of that of the 19th-century German philosopher, Friedrich Nietzsche, whom Lawrence read well in his youth and who must have been another inspirational source for the 'dark sun' topos. As Cecilia Björkén rightly indicates in her book on Lawrence and Nietzsche, 'Zarathustra's great aim' in *Thus Spoke Zarathustra* 'is to find the sun at midnight' (Björkén 226): after Zarathustra wakes from a long sleep he says that 'the *brightness of midnight* was all around me, loneliness crouched beside her; and as a third, the rasping stillness of death, the worst of my friends' (*Thus Spoke* 117) (italics mine). In other words, he is filled with new life after he died to the old self: he experiences midnight sun. At the end of the book Zarathustra 'left his cave, glowing and strong, like a *morning sun* that comes out of *dark* mountains' (281) (italics mine). Thus, Lawrence's 'dark sun' image sounds Nietzschean, too, as Björkén suggests.

Finally, in the connection with the 'dark sun' image, one might argue that an image of another English poet of the 17th century should be considered: Milton's 'darkness visible' in *Paradise Lost*. But it does not seem to be relevant here, because his 'darkness visible' refers to the darkness in the inferno into which Satan fell: it entirely lacks God's blessed light, for Milton says that: there 'peace / And rest can never dwell, hope never comes' (Frye 7), whereas the darkness of both Lawrence and the metaphysical poets symbolizes divine darkness – quite contrary to that 'darkness visible' in hell, which lacks divinity. In addition, 'the dark sun' is a combined symbol of divine darkness and divine light.

Notes

1. See the two images: 'the sun is dark' in *The Ladybird* (*FCDL* 180) and 'the dark sun '(*PS* 123).
2. As for this hymn, see also Parrinder, pp. 158–60.
3. The first two hymns in the hymnal might have been sung by Lawrence at the Congregational church in Eastwood while he was young. Although the hymnal is not *The Bristol Tune Book* (1863, 1876, 1881) which he refers to in 'Hymns in a Man's Life' (*LEA* 133) and which he certainly used, the former might have been used in hymn-singing at the 'Congo',

too, because a Congregational church was able to choose from a range of hymn books. The third hymn might have been known to Lawrence, too, since I speculate that he might have learned Methodist hymns from his mother – who was a Methodist before her marriage – and that the third hymn would have been among them. See also Lawrence's connection with Methodism through John Newton, his great-grandfather and a Wesleyan hymn composer (Sagar, *The Life* 11). I owe this note on hymn books to suggestions by Professor Erik Routley, Mr. Peter Preston (staff tutor in literature at the University of Nottingham) and Mr. John A. Parkinson, former senior research assistant of the British Library. I am, of course, responsible for any errors in the note.

4. See also Immoos, pp. 492–3; 35–6.

5. As for Murray's work, however, Kalnins says that 'DHL read the later version' ('Introduction' 18).

CHAPTER 2

LAWRENCE'S 'THE SHIP OF DEATH' AND OTHER POEMS IN *THE LAST POEMS NOTEBOOK*

i

Usually 'The Ship of Death' is related to *Sketches of Etruscan Places* and interpreted as a poem of the after-life. In this case it is also taken into consideration in justification of the interpretation that it was written just before Lawrence's death.

I do not disagree with those critics who maintain this interpretation[1] as far as the after-life theme is concerned. Yet, it seems to me also – as it does to another group of critics[2] – that the poem has another possibility of interpretation: it is a poem of 'spiritual death' [3] and resurrection here on earth, not in an after-life. To use Lawrence's words in *Apocalypse*, it is a poem of 'mystic death' (104) and resurrection in the flesh.

This 'mystic death' is characteristic not only of the pagan religion which Lawrence refers to in the book (*A* 104) but also of Christianity itself. The aim of this chapter is to relate Lawrence's 'mystic death' in 'The Ship of Death' and other poems in *The Last Poems Notebook* with that of Christian mystics, especially St. John of the Cross.

It is well known that Lawrence was brought up in Congregationalism and owed much to Congregational hymns, as seen in 'Hymns in a Man's Life' (*LEA* 130–34). However, several of his last poems – including 'The Ship of Death' – show that his experience of 'mystic death' reminds us of that of Catholic mystics. It seems probable that Lawrence in these poems stands close to them, though he is not conscious of it. Perhaps Robert A. Durr is the first scholar who has pointed out, though briefly, a similarity between Lawrence's 'The Ship of Death' and the anonymous 14th-century English mystic priest's *The Cloud of Unknowing* (Durr 109). My discussion will add something more to his brief allusion from a different angle.

ii

There are several poems in which Lawrence meditates on 'oblivion' or 'silence': 'Silence', 'Song of Death', 'The End, the Beginning', 'Sleep and Waking', 'Fatigue', 'Forget', 'Know-all', 'Tabernacle', 'Temples', 'Shadows', 'Change' and 'Phoenix'. As you will notice, all these poems except 'Silence' are arranged in this order at the end of *The Last Poems Notebook*. It seems that to this line of 'oblivion' or 'silence' come 'Invocation to the Moon,' 'Bavarian Gentians' and 'The Ship of Death'.

Sandra M. Gilbert comments on 'Bavarian Gentians', saying that:

> But in 'Bavarian Gentians', more than in any of his other works – perhaps even more than in the later 'Ship of Death' – Lawrence was trying to fit his mind to an experience that is by definition 'unimaginable' (Hough 214) and the tools he used were therefore those instruments of impossibility, paradox and oxymoron (...) At the centre of his field of vision (or, more properly, his field of intuition) was a phenomenological paradox: the impossible experience itself. (Gilbert 298)

Is the world of the poem 'the impossible experience'? And is Lawrence 'trying to fit his mind to an experience that is by definition 'unimaginable'?

In my opinion the world is quite imaginable and possible, because I think that the poem deals with his inner journey towards the dark or the world of oblivion by using the images of Pluto, of Persephone and of gentians. They are poetic instruments for describing the soul's journey.

While in 'Invocation to the Moon' Lawrence invokes the moon so that she might give him life, in 'Bavarian Gentians' he invokes not the moon but the dark silent world so that he can go down there. Why does he invoke the dark world or the moon in the dark silent night? Because the dark is the unfathomable source of life (and the moon is a life-transmitter from it in 'Invocation to the Moon') and by returning to it man is 'healed' and made 'whole' ('Invocation to the Moon', *Poems* 609).

And also the dark world is the world of 'oblivion' as well as 'of life supreme': in 'New Heaven and Earth' in *Look! We Have Come Through!* he tells us 'the black oblivion' which he experienced. In the poem there is his real experience of 'Sightless and strong oblivion':

> Sightless and strong oblivion in utter life takes possession of me!
> The unknown, strong current of life supreme
> drowns me and sweeps me away and holds me down
> to the sources of mystery, in the depths,
> extinguishes there my risen resurrected life
> and kindles it further at the core of utter mystery. (*Poems* 214)

But in 'Bavarian Gentians' he sings his own aspiration for the dark: he does not really sink down into it. Only imaginatively he aspires to sink there:

> let me guide myself with the blue, forked torch of this flower
> down the darker and darker stairs (...). (*Poems* 611)

Therefore it is purely an imaginative world, an imaginative journey of the soul. Or to use David Cavitch's words, 'the world of fantasy' (Cavitch 213) that he describes. Similarly, 'Invocation to the Moon' is an imaginative world in which he aspires to the life-sparkle of the moon and it does not represent the felt experience of being 'healed' and made 'whole'. Since there is the unknown world of mystery, it is at once imaginative – as seen in the two poems, and intuitively even possible – as in *Birds, Beasts and Flowers* – to sink down into through natural objects, say, flowers or animals. ('Snake', for example, shows his intuition, though momentarily, that the snake is: a king of the underworld, 'one of the lords / Of life' (*Poems* 305). In 'Medlars and Sorb-apples' he is intuitively in oneness with the dark world where the soul is 'like a flame blown whiter and whiter' (*Poems* 236).

And *The Last Poems Notebook* shows that he actually sank into oblivion. In 'Silence' he says:

> Ah! the holy silence – it is meet!
> It is very fitting! there is nought beside!
> For now we are passing through the gate, stilly,
> in the sacred silence of gates (...) (*Poems* 613)

This 'silence' is not what he was merely imagining or thinking about but what he really experienced, and out of the experience he wrote the poem in these images.

We can feel silence around us to some extent but the silence which Lawrence felt, as *The Last Poems Notebook* shows, is much different from that which we usually feel. It might be called the silence of sacred dimension: it is the silence which he felt by forgetting every earthly distracting idea. Because he says:

> Huge, huge roll the peals of the thundrous laugh
> huge, huger, huger and huger pealing
> till they mound and fill and all is fulfilled of God's last and greatest
>   laugh
> till all is soundless and senseless, a tremendous body of silence
> *enveloping even the edges of the thought waves,*
> *enveloping even me, who hear no more,*
> *who am embedded in a shell of silence,*
> *of silence, lovely silence*
> of endless and living silence
> of holy silence (...) (*Poems* 613) (italics mine)

'In the waking stage', as Chaman Nahal says, 'the mind is ever busy in weaving its web of fantasies' (Nahal 248). Hence: 'the barbed-wire entanglement / of his own ideas and his own mechanical devices' ('Terra incognita', *Poems* 575).

But notice the italicized words of the above extract. There 'even the edges of the thought waves' are gone. Lawrence has only one awareness of 'endless and living silence' and every other consciousness is thrown away. He feels only the great silence which he says is 'holy silence'.

This 'silence' does not envelop 'the edges of the thought waves' unless you try to cease from knowing or hearing or seeing. Once you cease from knowing or forget the self: 'silence' will descend upon you, as a grace, as it were, 'enveloping even me, who hear no more'. The 'silence' is 'holy silence', that is, the silence of God. He 'break(s) me down to his own oblivion' ('Shadows', *Poems* 641). The 'breaking' might be called a grace from God. The importance of ceasing to know is frequently emphasized. In 'Know-all' he says:

> Man knows nothing
> till he *knows how not-to know* (…)
> The end of all knowledge is oblivion
> sweet, dark oblivion, when I *cease*
> *even from myself*, and am consummated. (*Poems* 639) (italics mine)

Again, in 'Temples', he says:

> Oh, what we want on earth
> is centres here and there of silence and forgetting,
> where we may *cease from knowing*, and, as far as we know,
> may *cease from being*
> in the sweet wholeness of oblivion. (*Poems* 640) (italics mine)

In a letter to Rolf Gardiner on 3 December 1926 Lawrence already referred
to the importance of 'a centre of silence':

> There needs a centre of silence, and a heart of darkness
> (…) We'll have to establish some spot on earth, that will be
> the fissure into the underworld, like the oracle at Delphos,
> where one can always come to. I will try to do it myself.
> (*L* v 591)

The 'centre of silence' is a place where 'we may cease from knowing' 'in
the sweet wholeness of oblivion'. Although he did not do it himself, the
idea continued until his death.

'Not-to-know' or to 'cease from knowing' is negation of knowing or
reasoning. To be 'soundless and senseless' in 'silence' implies negation
of hearing or the senses. Negation of seeing is told in 'The breath of life':

> But if you want to breathe deep, sumptuous life
> breathe all alone, in silence, in the dark,
> and *see nothing*. (*Poems* 612) (italics mine)[4]

To cease from knowing, to cease from hearing, to cease from seeing and
the ceasing of the other senses – these are to cease from being and this is,

in other words, spiritual death in the holy silence of God. For Lawrence as thought-adventurer it is the discovery of a world of a new dimension. But for those who know Christian mystics his new discovery can be said to be, generally speaking, viewed in relation to the old tradition of Christian mysticism. A striking similarity might be pointed out between Lawrence's 'endless and living' and 'holy silence' and the 'divine silence' of St. John of the Cross, who says:

> The spirit that is indeed pure concerns not itself with advert-
> ence to exterior things, or with human respects, but inwardly,
> alone and withdrawn from all forms, and in delectable tran-
> quillity, it communes with God, for the knowledge of Him is
> in Divine silence. (Peers III: 222)

Whereas Lawrence says 'an absolute, utter forgetting / and a ceasing to know, a perfect ceasing to know / and a silent, sheer cessation of all awareness' ('The End, the Beginning', *Poems* 638), St. John of the Cross says that: the soul rejoices 'at having arrived at the height of perfection, which is union with God by the road of spiritual negation' (Campbell 11) and the anonymous author of *The Cloud of Unknowing* says likewise that: 'everything must be hidden under (the) cloud of forgetting' for the love of God (*The Cloud* 59).

Now, how do we feel 'the holy silence'? It is not to be felt by the senses but by the soul. In 'Silence', as quoted above, there is a line: 'For now we are passing through the gate, stilly', in which the word 'we' means the soul. Therefore the soul is passing through the gate of 'silence'.

The soul is the place where the silence of God is felt. It is worthwhile to remember 'Belief':

> Forever nameless
> Forever unknown
> Forever unconceived
> Forever unrepresented
> yet forever felt in the soul. (*Poems* 536)

An 18th-century English (and Protestant) mystic, William Law, gives us a more accurate explanation of the place of God's habitation. He says that the bottom of the soul is that place:

> Thy natural *Senses* cannot possess God, or unite Thee to Him, nay thy inward Faculties of *Understanding, Will* and *Memory*, can only reach after God, but cannot be the Place of his Habitation in Thee. But there is a *Root* or *Depth* in Thee, from whence all these Faculties come forth. (…) This Depth is called the *Centre*, the *Fund* or *Bottom* of the Soul. This Depth is the *Unity*, the *Eternity*, I had almost said, the *Infinity* of the Soul; for it is so infinite, that nothing can satisfy it, or give it any Rest, but the Infinity of God. (Law 28–9) (italics Law's)[5]

Although Lawrence never used the words 'the Centre, the Fund or Bottom of the Soul', to 'cease from knowing' and 'to cease from myself' mean, in Law's words, to return to 'the Centre' where the silence of God is felt.

That a tremendous body of silence envelops 'even the edges of the thought waves' is the death of the old self in God's oblivion. After the death comes the new self, the new-born self out of this, new-created by God:

> And if tonight my soul may find her peace
> in sleep, and sink in good oblivion,
> and in the morning wake like a new-opened flower
> then I have been dipped again in God, and new-created.
> ('Shadows', *Poems* 640)

'Sleep', here, means not only actual or physical sleep but also 'spiritual sleep' or 'mystical sleep' (Johnston 54).

In 'Phoenix' there is another good image of the resurrection into the new self after the death of the old one:

> The phoenix renews her youth
> only when she is burnt, burnt alive, burnt down
> to hot and flocculent ash. (*Poems* 642)

If life is renewed by being 'dipped into oblivion' and you will be 'like the eagle, / immortal bird' (*Poems* 641–42), then your life will be a god-like flame of life. And the first four poems of *Last Poems* (and *The Last Poems Notebook*) also deal with this theme. 'The Greeks Are Coming', 'The Argonauts', 'Middle of the World' and 'For the heroes are dipped in Scarlet', as Elizabeth Cipolla points out, 'reflect the 'morning wonder' of the world' (Cipolla 104): that is, the godly life-flame new-created. Since the theme is Lawrence's lifelong one, we may say that it is incorporated in *Last Poems* as a final opportunity, and 'The Ship of Death' is not unrelated with this endeavour.

iii

This theme is also embodied in 'The Ship of Death'. But it seems that it is outstandingly different from these four poems, from 'Invocation to the Moon' and from 'Bavarian Gentians' and from 'Phoenix'. Like 'Invocation to the Moon' and 'Bavarian Gentians', as seen above, 'The Greeks Are Coming', 'The Argonauts', 'Middle of the World', 'For the heroes are dipped in Scarlet' and 'Phoenix' represent imaginative experience, not actual or felt experience. In writing them Lawrence uses images appropriate for the imaginative world and these poems do not present his real and total experience of the negation of all images and ideas, or the old self, as far as their contents are concerned.

However, 'The Ship of Death' does unfold that experience of the negation of them.[6] This is most evidently shown in sections VII and VIII. And when we compare section VII with its corresponding lines of 'Ship of Death' in *The 'Nettles' Notebook* (*Poems* 594–97), it will be much clearer that Lawrence actually had the experience of the negation and also that he was more serene in the negation in 'The Ship of Death' than in 'Ship of Death'. I will show this soon.

The necessity of the negation of the old self written in 'The Ship of Death' is already implied in those preceding 'machine' poems, in which he says that evil is rampant and life is in peril:

> Only the human being, absolved from kissing and strife
> goes on and on and on, without wandering
> fixed upon the hub of the ego
> going, yet never wandering, fixed, yet in motion (…)
> ('Death is not Evil, Evil is Mechanical', *Poems* 627)

25

Therefore it is time that the old self died. It seems to me that the death of the old self and its renewal is most beautifully written in 'The Ship of Death' among all his poems.

The opening section is an announcement of the necessity of the death of 'the fallen self' with an autumn image, which is familiar with Lawrence as a symbol for the old self to die. And then in the third section Lawrence ponders if it will be worthwhile to commit suicide in order to escape from the death on the air. The answer is: 'Surely not so!' (*Poems* 630).

Instead of committing suicide he proposes to take 'the longest journey, to oblivion'. That is: to 'die the death, the long and painful death / that lies between the old self and the new'. (*Poems* 631) This 'death' will be called spiritual death or mystic death as we referred to before. In section VII the journey of death begins. And:

> There is no port, there is nowhere to go
> only the deepening black darkening still
> blacker upon the soundless, ungurgling flood
> darkness at one with darkness, up and down
> and sideways utterly dark, so there is no direction any more.
>
> And the little ship is there; yet she is gone.
> She is not seen, for there is nothing to see her by.
> She is gone! gone! and yet
> somewhere she is there.
> Nowhere! (*Poems* 632)

This is the process of forgetting the old self. It is not only the process of imaginatively drawing nearer and nearer to the state of actual death, but also the 'mystic death' which Lawrence is going through. And, the more the self forgets itself the darker it becomes in its depth. He says this in the lines: 'only the deepening black darkening still' and 'darkness at one with darkness'.

The self is hidden under the 'cloud of forgetting', to use the words of *The Cloud of Unknowing*. In the above extract Lawrence says that the ship of death comes to 'Nowhere'. 'Nowhere' is the point in which the old self has died (and then will be renewed). It will remind us of a contemplative piece of advice in *The Cloud of Unknowing*. The author of the book advises his disciples to go to 'nowhere' spiritually:

> 'Well' you will say, 'where am I to be? Nowhere, according to you!' And you will be quite right! 'Nowhere' is where I want you. Why, when you are 'nowhere' physically, you are 'everywhere' spiritually (…) Let go this 'everywhere' and 'everything' in exchange for this 'nowhere and this 'nothing'. (*The Cloud* 134–35)

His point is that the old self comes to 'nowhere' and 'nothing' so that the soul will know God.

In 'The Ship of Death' the depth of darkness is expressed in images of darkness which are laid one after the other, and the darkness comes to its culmination in section VIII:

> And everything is gone, the body is gone
> completely under, gone, entirely gone.
> The upper darkness is heavy on the lower,
> between them the little ship
> is gone
> she is gone.
>
> It is the end, it is oblivion. (*Poems* 632)

Since the old self is entirely forgotten – that is, thrown away and thus purified in this darkness – it might be said to be in the 'dark night' ('noche oscura') (Peers I: 329, 380; Campbell 10) of the soul in the words of St. John of the Cross, who says that the 'dark night' is 'spiritual night' of purification (Peers I: 456).

In the process of forgetting the self here, Lawrence does not suffer from such agony as is felt in 'Ship of Death' and his soul is much calmer and more serene in 'The Ship of Death' than in 'Ship of Death'. This will be exemplified by comparing section VII of 'The Ship of Death' with its corresponding part of 'Ship of Death', where the following lines read:

> Over the sea, over the farthest sea,
> on the longest journey,
> past the jutting rocks of shadow
> past the lurking, octopus arms of *agonised memory*,
> past the strange whirlpools of *remembered greed,*
> through the dead weed of *a life-time's falsity,*

'my soul' is 'taking the longest journey' (*Poems* 596) (italics mine). It is not so easy a task to forget the self in the journey of forgetting because, even if you try to do so – as Lawrence says: 'agonised memory' will come up to you, like 'octopus arms', 'remembered greed' will annoy you, like 'dead weed'. The lines above betray that Lawrence went them through and that he was once really agonized by them.

Going through this, he went to: 'the core / of sheer oblivion and of utter peace' ('Ship of Death', *Poems* 596). Though 'The Ship of Death' does not tell us: 'lovely peace, most lovely lapsing / of this my soul into the plasm of peace' as explicitly as in 'Ship of Death', yet it shows that his soul reaches a deeper level of darkness or oblivion than in 'Ship of Death', because in the former the soul suffers no more from 'agonised memory', 'remembered greed' and 'a lifetime's falsity' and it does go beyond the point where they assail it. It is freed from them; hence there is more calmness and serenity in the soul in 'The Ship of Death'.

'It is the end, it is oblivion' – this is the point in which there is no distracting idea or desire of the old self. It implies that the soul is entirely in the sweetness of oblivion, oblivion of God. In 'Forget' Lawrence says:

> To be able to forget is to be able to yield
> To god who dwells in deep oblivion.
> Only in sheer oblivion are we with God. (*Poems* 639)

Therefore, the soul which comes to 'the end' or 'oblivion' might well be said to be in the oblivion of God and with him in the sheer oblivion.

This state of the soul might be compared with that of St. John of the Cross:

Without support, yet well supported,
Though in *pitch-darkness*, with no ray,
Entirely I am burned away.

　　……　……　……
Though good and bad in me are neighbours
He turns their difference to naught
Then both into Himself, so sweetly,
And with *a flame* so fine and fragrant
Which now I feel in me completely
Reduce my being, till *no vagrant*
Vestige of my own self can stay.
And wholly I am burned away. (Campbell 82–3) (italics mine)

This 'pitch-darkness' ('a oscuras viviendo') is quite similar to Lawrence's 'deepening black darkening still', and the latter darkness sounds like that 'dark night' of the soul which the former really is. And in section VIII of 'The Ship of Death', as in the above extract, 'no vagrant / Vestige of my own self' ('sin quedar cosa') must have been felt in that oblivion. To put it in a different way, the old self has been burned away or perished there. Whereas Lawrence writes 'It is the end, it is oblivion', St. John of the Cross writes:

I intreated him to kill me
Since he'd wounded me so sore.
And I leaped into his fire
Knowing it would burn me more.

　　……　……　…… .
In myself for you I *perished*
Yet through you revive once more (...)
　　　　(Campbell 78–9) (italics mine)

This is St. John of the Cross's knowledge of God. And he said, as we saw above, that 'the knowledge of Him is in divine silence'. It seems to me that this 'divine silence' is equivalent to what Dionysius the Areopagite called 'divine Darkness' (*The Divine Names* 192) which is 'the unapproachable light in which God is said to dwell' (Johnston 33). A road to it is, again in

St. John of the Cross's words, 'the road of spiritual negation'. Lawrence seemed to have experienced this sort of 'divine silence' or 'divine Darkness' through 'the road of spiritual negation' in his own way and wrote the finest piece, 'The Ship of Death', being based upon the deepest mystical experience in life.

After the death of the old self in God one revives once more. St. John of the Cross says in the above quotation: 'In myself for you I perished / Yet through you revive once more' ('En mi por ti me moria / Y por ti resucitaba').

In another song he says:

> Oh *lamps of fiery blaze*
> To whose refulgent fuel
> The deepest caverns of my soul grow bright,
> Late blind with gloom and haze,
> But in this strange renewal
> Giving to the belov'd both *heat and light.*
> (Campbell 28–9) (italics mine)

And he goes on saying that his soul is filled with 'peace' ('¡Cuan manso y amoroso') (Campbell 28–9).

Lawrence writes the renewal process in sections IX and X where similar images of brightness and peace to those of St. John of the Cross are found. In section IX he says:

> Ah wait, wait, for there's the dawn,
> the cruel dawn of coming back to life
> out of oblivion.
>
> … … … .
> Wait, wait! even so, a flush of yellow
> and strangely, O chilled wan soul, a flush of rose. (*Poems* 633)

Once the fallen self has died in the 'oblivion of God' it is simultaneously renewed by him. The renewed life is, in Lawrence's words, 'a stark flame' of life (*A* 104). Its colours are yellow and red. 'A flush of yellow' and 'a flush of rose' come from 'out of eternity' (*Poems* 632–33) and shine on the chilled wan soul in these colours. They are very similar to those of 'lamps of fiery blaze' ('lámparas de fuego') which brighten the soul and of its 'heat and light' ('calor y luz') in St. John of the Cross's poem because the colours in both cases symbolize eternal life.

If there is 'a flush of yellow' or 'of rose' coming out of eternity there must be the ultimate source of light from which the light issues forth: this source must be in the dark because, when the soul has sunk completely into the dark, out of the very depth of darkness there comes that flush of yellow or of rose. What is this source of light? Although Lawrence never uses the word God in 'The Ship of Death' the source might well be guessed to be God in 'divine Darkness.' Instead of the word God, Lawrence uses other images for eternal light or life in other places. One of them is 'the sun of suns' in *Pansies* (*Poems* 416 ('Underneath'), 417('The Primal Passions'), 430 ('Glory'), 456 ('Space', 'Sun-men'), etc.) and another one is 'the dark sun' in *The Plumed Serpent* (123) or *The Ladybird* (*FCDL* 180). Since 'the sun of suns' or 'the dark sun' is both ultimately invisible and the unknown life source, it is in the dark: paradoxically, it shines in the dark. The flush of yellow or rose, probably coming from the sun of suns, is shining in the dark.

This is quite in parallel with the case of St. John of the Cross; 'a flame' ('su llama'), obviously originating from God, was burning in that 'pitch-darkness.' He calls such firelight 'divine and dark spiritual light' (Peers I: 394). The 'flame' is, needless to say, a symbolic fire of God's life, and similarly Lawrence's 'flush' or 'the sun of suns' is symbolic of God's light or life of eternity. These images in both cases can be called archetypal symbols for eternal life or light and, in this Jungian respect at least, Lawrence has a very close resemblance to St. John of the Cross (and to Dionysius the Areopagite, too, who calls the divine light shining in the dark 'the ray of that divine Darkness') (*The Divine Names* 192).

These colours are neither felt by the self-centred self, 'the fallen self' nor possessed by the senses, because they are far beyond it and beyond the senses. They are only felt in the soul, since the ultimately unknown is – as we saw above – 'forever felt in the soul', or at the 'bottom of the soul'. To express this differently: they are seen not by the physical eye but by the eye of the soul or the third eye, so to speak. The ship of death is, as it were, journeying over the ego through and beyond the unconscious to the centre of the soul where 'out of eternity' there shines forth 'a thread' (*Poems* 632) of the divine light which awakens the third eye and revives the soul by piercing it in a 'cruel' way (*Poems* 633).

> When the soul is new-created, naturally it has peace:
>
> … … … .
>
> and the frail soul steps out, into her house again
> filling the heart with peace. (section X, *Poems* 633)

Tom Marshall considers 'her house' to be a body of after-life (Marshall 221). It seems to me, however, that the house means not only a body of after-life but that body in life here in which the soul or the stark flame of life dwells. And the 'peace' in the line above, therefore, seems to mean such peace as is felt by St. John of the Cross in communion with God here on earth as well as peace in the after-life.

iv

It will be concluded, then, that 'The Ship of Death' is a poem of death and renewal of the self. In it, the process of the dying of the old self means its returning to that centre of the soul where there is 'immediate contact with God' or 'Contact with the sun of suns' ('The Primal Passions', *Poems* 417), and is therefore followed by its renewal process. Both processes are what Christian mystics experienced. In saying this I do not argue that Lawrence was a Catholic mystic like St. John of the Cross, the anonymous author of *The Cloud of Unknowing* or Dionysius the Areopagite. I only say that he was a man of 'the mystical journey towards God' (Carter 8) like the Catholic mystics, and several poems of *Last Poems* tell us that in them he stands close to those mystics, unawares (Lawrence's earlier mystic experience – which will develop into that similar to theirs – can be traced phase after phase especially from *Look! We Have Come Through!* onwards, as we have seen in the previous chapter). In his way he had, like them, the mystic death and 'the mystic experience of ecstasy in rebirth' (*A* 166) of which 'The Ship of Death' is the best evidence at the end of his life. Therefore, it is possible to appreciate this poem and several others by relating them to the tradition of Christian mysticism, unpopular as such an appreciation has been among Lawrentian scholars. [7] In 1924 he said in an essay 'On Being

Religious' that 'the real problem for humanity' was, 'how shall man put himself into relation to God, into a living relation?' In other words, 'how shall Man *find* God?' (Lawrence's italics) (*RDP* 189–90). And, near the end of his life, according to Brewster, he also said, 'I wish to realize my relation with Him' (Brewster 224). 'The Ship of Death' seems to be the best answer to his own question.

Notes

1. de Sola Pinto, pp. 19–20; Panichas, p. 204; Cipolla, pp. 111–15; Marshall, pp. 216–21; Suzuki, p. 274.
2. Cavitch, p. 217; Nahal, pp. 245–50; Durr, pp. 109–10; Knight, p. 220.; Gilbert, pp. 307–12; Meyers, p. 86.
3. Salgado, p. 244. Quoted by permission of the author.
4. Cf. 'Travel is over', *Poems*, p. 571.
5. For this citation I am indebted to the advice of Dr Marcus Walsh and to Bede Griffiths: *Return to the Centre*, p. 5, where the passage is cited.
6. This sort of negation experience is shown in *Look! We Have Come Through!* for the first time in his poetic career. See e.g., 'In the Dark', 'New Heaven and Earth', 'Manifesto', etc. A similar tone echoes in Birkin's words: 'I should like to go with you *nowhere*. It would be rather wandering just to *nowhere*. That's the place to get to – *nowhere*. One wants to wander away from the world's somewhere, into our own *nowhere*' (*WL* 315) (italics mine). Akinobu Ohkuma indicates in his recent book that Birkin's 'nowhere' in this passage suggests his mystic 'via negativa' experience, which is similar to that detailed in *The Cloud of Unknowing* (Ohkuma 152–3).
7. Bethan Jones (in her recent book) discusses 'The Ship of Death' as 'the most evidently Etruscan poem' by relating it to *Sketches of Etruscan Places*, yet not mentioning any possibility of Lawrence's mystic experience in the poem (Jones 63–6), although she discusses 'elements of pre-Socratics' in detail (93–116). Although Ohkuma – in the above book – demonstrates an insightful analysis of Lawrence's 'via negativa' mysticism in sexual scenes in such novels as *Sons and Lovers*, *The Rainbow*, *Women in Love*, *The Plumed Serpent* or *Lady Chatterley's Lover*, or the poem 'New Heaven and Earth' (Ohkuma 107–63) he does not, strangely enough, refer to Lawrence's 'via negativa' mysticism

in meditation in 'The Ship of Death'. C. J. P. Lee, on the other hand, compares, though just briefly, the 'via negativa' experience of this poem with Kate's similar experience in *The Plumed Serpent* by referring to St. John of the Cross (Lee 61–3), but does not make a full discussion of the topic.

CHAPTER 3

D. H. LAWRENCE: THE BIBLE AND THE MYSTICS

i

In his letter to the Reverend Robert Reid of 27 March 1911 (*L* i 244), Lawrence says that the Bible was his 'flesh and blood'. Indeed 'his writing can be read fruitfully as an interpretation of the Bible, a midrashic commentary and a creative exegesis of it', as Terry R. Wright indicates in his *D. H. Lawrence and the Bible* (12).

Lawrence's poems also contain many references to and creative interpretations of the Bible (Wright 245–51). For example, in 'The Hands of God' (*The Last Poems Notebook*), Lawrence says:

> It is a fearful thing to fall into the hands of the living God.
> But it is a much more fearful thing to fall from out of them.
> (*Poems* 613)

The first line is taken word for word from the Bible (Hebrews 10:31), and his belief in the 'living God' is evident in this poem. Nevertheless, Lawrence cannot be called an orthodox Christian in the strictest sense because – as David Ellis indicates – Lawrence does not believe in 'an anthropomorphic deity' in the period of *Last Poems* but believes, instead, in 'some presence' which is 'more akin to pagan or animist creative force' (Ellis 520). Indeed, Lawrence considers Christ to be only one of 'all sorts of gods' whom 'humanity has ever known', as he expressed in his poem 'All sorts of gods':

> There's all sorts of gods, all sorts and every sort,
> and every god that humanity has ever known is still a god today
> the African queer ones and Scandinavian queer ones,
> The Greek beautiful ones, the Phoenician ugly ones, the Aztec
>   hideous ones,

> goddesses of love, goddesses of dirt, excrement-eaters or lily
>   virgins,
> Jesus, Buddha, Jehovah and Ra, Egypt and Babylon,
> all the gods, and you see them all if you look, alive and moving
>   today (...) (*Poems* 579)

Broadly speaking, Lawrence can be called a religious or mystic poet. In some poems he refers to darkness as mystic darkness, which enables the soul to be reborn, as is most evident in 'The Ship of Death' in which the soul takes the longest journey into 'darkness at one with darkness' where 'She is gone' (*Poems* 632). The 'darkness' in this poem can be attributed to three religious sources: the Bible, Greek mysticism and Christian mysticism. Mystic darkness in the Bible can be encountered, as we have seen in chapter 1 (Exodus 20:21, Psalms 18: 11 or Deuteronomy 4: 11–12). Needless to say, Lawrence must have been familiar with the biblical mystic darkness as God's dwelling place. This biblical darkness echoes in Lawrence's 'darkness' in 'The Ship of Death'.

Another echo can be found in the Greek mystics' experience of darkness which Lawrence discovered in John Burnet's *Early Greek Philosophy* (1892), where Burnet explains that Heraclitus and Parmenides felt 'Darkness' as the great life source (Burnet 132; 186). Lawrence read Burnet's book in 1915 and was very impressed with Greek mystic philosophy, as he says in a letter of 1915: 'I have been wrong, much too Christian, in my philosophy. These early Greeks have clarified my soul. I must drop all about God' (*L* ii 364). There would therefore seem to be a connection between the Greek mystics' 'Darkness' and that found in Lawrence's in 'The Ship of Death'.

A third echo may be said to come from Christian mystics whose mystic experience is discussed by William Rauf Inge in his *Christian Mysticism* (1899). Inge indicates that the 4th-century Syrian mystic Dionysius the Areopagite experienced 'divine darkness' or 'a deep but dazzling light' (Inge 109); the 14th-century English mystic Walter Hilton experienced 'darkness' as the 'herald of a brighter dawn' (200); the 16th-century Spanish mystic St. John of the Cross experienced three stages of night of the soul before 'the dawn of the supernatural state' (227). The mystic darkness of these three figures bears similarities to Lawrence's own.

William Inge (Dean of St. Paul's) was Burnet's contemporary, and Lawrence did read Inge's *The Philosophy of Plotinus* (1918) in 1929, as Edward Nehls and David Ellis indicate (Nehls 403; Ellis 516). Perhaps Lawrence had read the book three years earlier, for Clifford refers to Plotinus in *The First Lady Chatterley*, which was finished in 1926. Clifford, after listening to Mrs. Bolton's gossip for several hours, 'emerge(s) into the comparative Paradise of Plotinus' (*FSLC* 127). It is plausible to suggest that Lawrence may have read Inge's more well-known book – *Christian Mysticism* – around that time as well, though Nehls and Ellis do not mention it.

I wish to shed light here on the contribution of Inge's *Christian Mysticism* to the creation of Lawrence's poetic imagery of unconsciousness or darkness because, while Burnet's *Early Greek Philosophy* has often been referred to in past Lawrence studies, Inge's book has been overlooked.

ii

Burnet analyzed ancient Greet mysticism in *Early Greek Philosophy,* and Inge analyzed Christian mysticism in *Christian Mysticism*. Though both works are important in order to understand Lawrence's poetry – especially *The 'Nettles' Notebook* and *The Last Poems Notebook* – I will focus on Inge's *Christian Mysticism* rather than *The Philosophy of Plotinus* because the former provides us with several interesting clues which help us to appreciate Lawrence's later poems, notably 'The Heart of Man', 'Terra incognita', 'Death is not Evil, Evil is Mechanical' and – above all – 'The Ship of Death'.

Before we consider 'The Ship of Death' it is useful first of all to give a passing mention of the affinity which exists between Lawrence and the German Romantic novelist Jean Paul Richter (1763–1825) (whom Inge discusses in *Christian Mysticism*) in order to show Inge's contribution to Lawrence's poetic imagery of the unconscious. In *Christian Mysticism*, Inge quotes the following observation of Richter concerning the unconscious:

> We attribute far too small dimensions to the rich empire of
> ourselves, if we omit from it the unconscious region which
> resembles *a great dark continent.* The world which our

memory peoples only reveals, in its revolution, a few luminous points at a time, while its immense and teeming mass
remains in shade. (Inge 30–31) (italics mine)

To give poetic expression to Richter's phrase 'a great dark continent' – the
realm of the unconscious – would arguably produce images very akin to
those Lawrence uses: 'the pulsating continent / of the heart of man' ('The
Heart of Man'), or 'vast realms of consciousness still undreamed of' ('Terra
incognita'). In 'The Heart of Man', Lawrence says:

There is the other universe, of the heart of man
that we know nothing of, that we dare not explore.
A strange grey distance separates
our pale mind still from the *pulsating continent*
of the heart of man. (*Poems* 522) (italics mine)

In the next stanza Lawrence says that the 'continent' is 'darker still than
Congo or Amazon' (*Poems* 522). In 'Terra incognita' Lawrence puts it in a
slightly different way:

There are *vast realms of consciousness still undreamed of*
vast ranges of experiences, like the humming of unseen harps,
we know nothing of, within us. (*Poems* 575) (italics mine)

The 'vast realms of consciousness still undreamed of' are terra incognita,
as the title of the poem suggests. Lawrence may well have been inspired
by Richter's observation of the unconscious, as found in Inge's *Christian
Mysticism*[1].

Another and more important example of poetic inspiration – which
Inge's book may have provided Lawrence with – is the experience of
Christian mystics such as Walter Hilton, Dionysius the Areopagite, and
St. John of the Cross. Inge explains:

The way in which Hilton conceives the 'truly mystical darkness' of Dionysius (the Areopagite) is very interesting. As a
psychic experience, it has its place in the history of the inner

life. The soul does enter into darkness, and the darkness is not fully dispelled in this world; 'thou art not there yet', as he says (…) The 'darkness' is felt to be only the herald of a brighter dawn: 'the darker the night, the nearer the true day'. (Inge 200)

The 'truly mystical darkness' of Dionysius the Areopagite is what Inge calls 'the divine darkness', which is 'dark through excess of light' or 'a deep but dazzling darkness' (Inge 109).

Hilton's or Dionysius the Areopagite's experience of 'darkness' and 'dawn' or 'dazzling darkness' reminds us of Lawrence's similar psychic experience (which he describes in 'The Ship of Death') in which the soul, after taking the longest journey, is finally lost in darkness and oblivion: 'She is gone. / It is the end, it is oblivion' (*Poems* 632) [2]. While Lawrence does not relate 'oblivion' to God in 'The Ship of Death', he does so in 'Forget': 'To be able to forget is to be able to yield / To god who dwells in deep oblivion. / Only in sheer oblivion are we with God' (*Poems* 639).

Lawrence's 'oblivion' seems to echo another Christian mystic, St. John of the Cross, who says that the soul – after three nights of spiritual purification – sinks into 'oblivion' before 'the dawn of the supernatural state'. Inge indicates:

In the 'third (that is, the deepest) night' – that of memory and will – the soul sinks into a holy inertia and *oblivion* (santa ociosidad y olvido) in which the flight of time is unfelt, and the mind is unconscious of all particular thoughts (…) It is the last watch of the night before the dawn of the supernatural state, in which the human faculties are turned into divine attributes, and by a complete transformation the soul – which was 'at the opposite extreme' to God – 'becomes, by participation, God'. (Inge 227) (italics mine)

In this connection Lawrence's 'oblivion' can also be related to a 14th-century anonymous English mystic's 'cloud of unknowing' though Inge, strangely enough, does not refer to this medieval mystic in *Christian Mysticism*. In *The Cloud of Unknowing* this anonymous mystic advises his disciples to arrive at the mystic state, where 'everything must be hidden under the cloud of unknowing' so that their souls know God (59).

He goes on to advise them to: 'let go this "everywhere" and "everything" in exchange for (the) nowhere' where the old self dies and the soul knows God (135). That is, everything must be forgotten or abandoned in complete darkness or oblivion for the love of God.

Just as St. John of the Cross's soul is visited by 'the dawn of the supernatural state' after oblivion, as Inge indicates, so is Lawrence's soul in 'The Ship of Death'. After the soul is gone in darkness, there comes 'the dawn' : 'there's the dawn, / the cruel dawn of coming back to life / out of oblivion'(*Poems* 633).

Lawrence then introduces the image of a 'house' as the dwelling place of the soul:

> And the little ship wings home, faltering and lapsing
> on the pink flood,
> and frail soul steps out, into her house again,
> filling the heart with peace. (*Poems* 633)

Lawrence's use of 'house' and 'soul' here seems to echo Hilton, because the latter uses the same 'house' image when advising Christian converts to awaken their souls to Christ when Christ is lost: 'Christ is lost, like the piece of money in the parable; but where? In thy house, that is, in thy soul' (quoted in Inge 199). In his poem Lawrence replaces Hilton's 'Christ' with light. Lawrence therefore employs Hilton's 'house' metaphor as the place where the newly reborn soul dwells, tailoring the image to suit his own needs.

Lawrence also transforms Hilton's 'disturbing noises' into various expressions in his poems, 'Terra incognita' and 'Ship of Death', which is a briefer version of 'The Ship of Death'. Hilton advises his followers to 'put away disturbing noises' in order to 'hear Him':

> First, however, find the image of sin, which thou bearest about
> with thee. It is no bodily thing, no real thing – only a lack of
> light or love. (Quoted in Inge 199)

Hilton's 'disturbing noises' is changed to: 'barbed-wire entanglement /of his own ideas and his mechanical devices' in 'Terra incognita' (*Poems* 575).

In 'Ship of Death' metaphorical expressions replacing Hilton's 'disturbing noises' are employed to describe the soul's inner journey: 'the lurking, octopus arms of agonised memory', 'the strange whirlpools of remembered greed', and 'the dead weed of a lifetime's falsity' (*Poems* 596). (See Chapter 2)

For Hilton, man's consciousness of sin must embrace the darkness: 'the darker the night is, the nearer is the true day'(quoted in Inge 199), so that when 'the night passeth away', 'the day dawneth'; and a 'flash of light shines the soul through the chinks of the wall of Jerusalem' (quoted in Inge 199).

For Lawrence, egocentric consciousness or 'obscene ego' ('Death is not Evil, Evil is Mechanical' (*Poems* 628)) must give way to darkness, so that when the soul sinks into darkness and oblivion a new 'dawn' will come 'out of eternity', as we have seen above. The soul then shines through 'a flush of yellow' or 'a flush of rose':

> And yet out of eternity, a thread
> separates itself on the blackness,
> a horizontal thread
> that fumes a little with pallor upon the dark (…)
> Wait, wait, even so, a flush of yellow
> and strangely, O chilled wan soul, a flush of rose. (*Poems* 632–3)

Just as Hilton uses the images of the 'dawn' and 'flash of light', Lawrence uses those of the 'dawn' and 'a flush of yellow' or 'a flush of rose'. While Hilton says the new light illuminates the soul 'through the chinks of the walls of Jerusalem', Lawrence says that it comes 'out of eternity'.

While Hilton, Dionysius the Areopagite and St. John of the Cross describe the process of the soul's death and rebirth in Christian mystical imagery, Lawrence describes a similar process of the soul's death and rebirth in his own mystical imagery. Lawrence's mystical experience is partly an echo of the experience of these Christian mystics, which Inge closely scrutinises in *Christian Mysticism*.

Although Lawrence's phraseology in *The Last Poems Notebook* is similar to Hilton's or other expressions used by the Christian mystics, it cannot be said that Lawrence's mystic experience is explainable only in Christian mystic terminology, because his experience also seems to be an echo of Greek mystic experience. In fact, 'The Ship of Death' never mentions God or Christ in the traditionally Christian sense.

Greek mystics, like Heraclitus and Parmenides, experienced mystical darkness (as John Burnet's *Early Greek Philosophy* demonstrates) and according to Toshihiko Izutsu's *Mystic Philosophy* Parmenides says that the soul is flooded by dazzling light after it sinks into complete darkness (see chapter 1). Parmenides's mystic experience of darkness and light is very close to Lawrence's mystic experience in 'The Ship of Death'. For both, the Christian God is absent.

Thus, Lawrence's mystic experience seems a mixture of Christian and Greek mystic experience. He is a mystic poet in his own way[3], immersing himself in the traditions of the Bible, Christian mysticism, and Greek mysticism. Or – to put it differently – Lawrence's poems referring to mystic darkness are closely intertexualized with the Bible and Christian writings and the writings of Greek mystics, crossing over their boundaries freely and creatively to produce his new poetic utterance.

Notes
1. Another source which Lawrence must have read is H. D. Thoreau's *Walden* (1854), in which he says: 'Direct your eye right inward, and you'll find / A thousand regions in your mind / Yet undiscovered. Travel then, and be / Expert in home-cosmography' (285–6).
2. Lawrence's interest in the soul's journey into darkness and its succeeding rebirth, that is, the so-called via negativa which was pursued by mystics such as Walter Hilton, Dionysius the Areopagite, St. John of the Cross etc., is already evident in 'St Matthew' in *Birds, Beasts and Flowers* (1923), in which he says: 'And I take the wings of the morning, to Thee, Crucified, Glorified. (…) / And (at evening) I must resume my nakedness like a fish, sinking down the dark reversion of night / Like a fish seeking the bottom, Jesus, ΙΧΘΥΣ (…)' (*Poems* 276).
3. See Stephen Taylor's 2001 essay 'Lawrence the Mystic', pp. 62–74. Though Taylor does not mention Robert A. Durr priority should be given to the latter in discussing Lawrence as a mystic because, as I indicated in my 1981 essay on 'The Ship of Death' (see Chapter 2), Durr was the

first scholar who observed the closeness between Lawrence's 'The Ship of Death' and the 14th-century anonymous English mystic's *The Cloud of Unknowing* (despite the fact that Durr did not closely analyse the relationship in his 1970 book) (109–10).

CHAPTER 4

LAWRENCE'S PAGAN GODS AND CHRISTIANITY

i

Every reader of Lawrence's novels notices that pagan gods or goddesses appear in some of them. Sometimes they are used as metaphors but at other times they are felt as living deities by characters in the novels. In this chapter I will concentrate on the latter use of gods and goddesses in his novels, because they are vitally important when we look at the characters' living relationships with nature.

Critics have paid perceptive attention to this topic previously. For example, Robert E. Gajdusek notes the significance of pagan gods in *The White Peacock* (Gajdusek 188–203); Dennis Jackson discusses Lawrence's 'old pagan vision' in *Lady Chatterley's Lover* (Jackson 260–71), and Michael Squires places both of those narratives in a tradition of 'pastoral novels' dating back to Theocritus or Virgil (Squires 178–81; 196–8). Another critic, Anja Viinikka, investigates Lawrence's 'mythopoeic vision' by focusing on 'ancient mythic elements, that is, 'Greek deities' (26) – in his short stories and novellas in the early 1920s. And K. J. Phillips in *Dying Gods in Twentieth-Century Fiction* considers Lawrence's *The Plumed Serpent*, 'The Woman Who Rode Away', *Lady Chatterley's Lover* and *The Man Who Died* (*The Escaped Cock*) as she discusses 'the dying gods (Lawrence uses) as metaphors for individuals or whole civilisations in need of rebirth' (138–9). But Phillips does not seem to be interested in the gods and goddesses whom protagonists feel as living deities. My aim here is to clarify a living relationship between protagonists and pagan deities in Lawrence's novels.

In his works there are two kinds of gods: those of European origin and those of non-European origin. When he deals with the former gods like Pan, dryads, or the spirit of England he seems to be at home with them, as is seen in associations between Annable and Pan, Cyril and the spirit of Nethermere or the dryads in *The White Peacock*; Lou and Pan in *St. Mawr*; Somers and the spirit of Cornwall in *Kangaroo*; and Mellors and Pan in *Lady Chatterley's Lover*. But Lawrence does not seem to be as comfortable with non-European gods such as Quetzalcoatl or the spirit of the Australian bush, as we see in Kate's ambiguous attitude toward Quetzalcoatl in *The Plumed Serpent* and in Somers's recoil from the threatening spirit of the Australian bush. This suggests that the deities of European origin appeal to his 'blood consciousness' more profoundly than those of non-European origin.

Why does he try to revive a sense of these deities in his works? It is because he wants to make people emotionally or intuitively vital by exposing them to the world of nature or the cosmos where the gods dwell. By doing so he sometimes tries to revitalize Christianity, too, because he believes that Christianity has become rigid and has lost vitality. Lawrence hopes that, by turning to the gods of nature, Christianity might be reinvigorated by a different life principle.

The following discussion focuses on six novels or novellas: *The White Peacock*, where Pan, dryads and a spirit of place first appear in a Christian context; *St. Mawr*, where Pan plays a more important role for its heroine than in any other work; *The Plumed Serpent* and *Kangaroo*, where non-European deities make the protagonists restless; and *Lady Chatterley's Lover* and *The Escaped Cock*, where Christianity and paganism meet and are reconciled.

ii

Although Cyril and all his friends in *The White Peacock* were once 'the children of the valley of Nethermere' (237), it is only Cyril who can apprehend such deities as 'dryads' or the 'spirit of place'. As he strolls through the wood of Nethermere he tells himself 'that the dryads were looking out for me from the wood's edge' (306). Or, while walking along the roads of Norwood, (far away from Nethermere) he is haunted by 'the spirit of some part of Nethermere':

> As I went along the quiet roads where the lamps in yellow
> loneliness stood among the leafless trees of the night I would
> feel the feeling of the dark, wet bit of path between the wood

meadow and the brooks. The spirit of that wild little slope to
the (Strelley) Mill would come upon me (…) (260)

The dryads – though of Greek origin – would appeal to English readers, for 'all the old Aryans', 'my ancestors', 'worshipped the tree', as Lawrence tells us in *Fantasia of the Unconscious* (86). In other words they felt a deity living in a tree when they worshipped it. Or 'the old Englishman', as he says in the essay 'Aristocracy', had a 'living, vital relation to the oak tree, a *mystic* relation' (Lawrence's italics): the 'last living vibration and power in pure connection, between man and tree' came down to the Englishman 'from the Druids' (*RDP* 372). As for the spirit of place, it is originally Celtic. The Celts believed in 'a spirit of place as well as spirits of their ancestors' (Imura 58: my translation). There is thus a mixture of Greek and Celtic deities in Cyril's blood consciousness.

Cyril's sharp intuition of 'dryads' or 'spirits of place', however, deteriorates when he uproots himself from the soil of Nethermere and becomes an urban dweller. Thereafter, the dryads no longer welcome him when he returns home. Instead they regard him as 'a stranger, an intruder' (*WP* 306). He is no longer a living part of the valley of Nethermere. His friend George (a farmer's son) is also excluded from the valley of Nethermere, for he has lost hope in his future as a farmer and turned his back on the farming life.

Compared with Cyril and George the character Annable is more deeply rooted in the soil of the forest, because he is quite content with his life as gamekeeper and has no intention of leaving. He is a contrasting figure to the young people and makes the story symmetrical, as Lawrence told Jessie Chambers (Chambers 117). When Cyril and his friends go to the wood Annable appears before them 'like some malicious Pan' (130), for he notices that they do not love the life of the wood. He believes that those who want to go into the wood should love its life. He is not, however, given full credit by Lawrence (who kills him off in an accident halfway through the novel). It is obvious that Lawrence is not as confident of Annable's role as he is of that of Mellors later, in *Lady Chatterley's Lover*. While Mellors insists that the mass of people 'should be alive and frisky and acknowledge the great god Pan' (*LCL* 300), Annable does not have such a firm belief in the forest god. He says only, 'Be a good animal, true to your animal instinct' (*WP* 147).

As long as he lives in the forest, however, Annable lives in harmony with its life and is even blessed by nature when he dies. When his coffin is carried through the fields elm-boughs and flowers show 'sympathy' for him:

> The bearers lift up the burden again, and the elm-boughs rattle along the hollow white wood, and the pitiful red clusters of elm-flowers sweep along it as if they whispered in sympathy– 'We are so sorry, so sorry – '; always the compassionate buds in their fulness of life bend down to comfort the dark man shut up there. (*WP* 157)

Thus, his life and death are seen as part of a natural cycle.

Annable is important in the novel not only because he is Pan-like, but also because he is an ex-curate. His former life as curate with Lady Christabel was not a happy one because, as he tells Cyril, she was too spiritual a woman and denied him his physical life. But his life with his new wife Proserpine (whose name reminds us of the goddess of the underworld) fills up the emptiness of his former life. The paganism (with which he is associated) does not, however, mean that he is not a Christian. Nowhere does he state his disbelief in Christianity, though he sometimes criticizes it by saying, 'The church is rotten' (*WP* 149).

In his first novel Lawrence seems to make a first immature attempt to reconcile Annable's two elements, pagan and Christian. The reconciliation motif is taken up again in *Lady Chatterley's Lover* and *The Escaped Cock*. Before we go on to the later fiction, however, there are two works in between where pagan gods are a dominant principle and Christianity withdraws: *St. Mawr* and *The Plumed Serpent*. They were written while Lawrence lived in New Mexico where 'the essential Christianity on which my character was established' was almost 'shattered' ('New Mexico', *MM* 176).

A firm belief in Pan is achieved by Lou Carrington in *St. Mawr*. While Lou's husband Rico is satisfied with his urban life she is discontented. She finds her human relations trivial and superficial, but when she sees a horse called St. Mawr she is awakened to its mysterious power. She senses the presence of Pan in the horse and feels she must 'worship' him (*StM* 31). The horse challenges her to choose either 'her ordinary, commonplace self' (*StM* 31) or the mysterious life of the horse, and she chooses the latter. She also associates Pan with the Welsh groom Lewis, who is quite different from her husband. Like John Thomas, Somers's closest friend in *Kangaroo*, Lewis is a man of rich Celtic imagination: he believes that 'fairies' are living in ash-trees, the people in the moon 'wash the air clean with moonlight', and the sky sends a message down to earth, 'whether we want it or not' (*StM* 107–9).

Lou buys the horse and goes back to America with the groom, her mother, and the servant Phoenix. She buys a ranch, where a great pine tree stands as 'guardian of the place (…) a bristling, almost demonish guardian' (*StM* 144). She is struck by 'the spirit that is wild' (*StM* 155) and decides to settle there: 'it's my mission to keep myself for the spirit that is wild, and has waited so long here: even waited for such as me. Now I've come! Now I am here. Now I am where I want to be: with the spirit that wants me' (*StM* 155). Lou's philosophy of serving this spirit is in direct contrast with Rico's or Mrs. Witt's obsession. Rico's domineering will is betrayed when he tries to control St. Mawr and is maimed by the horse. Mrs. Witt, having a 'morbid interest in other people and their doings' (*StM* 44), is also obsessed with a will to dominate them. Neither has 'respect' (*StM* 112) for the life of others.

Lou's blood consciousness is first roused by the Pan-like power of St. Mawr and Lewis, and then by the wild spirit of her mother country. It is what matters most to her now and neither Rico's nor Mrs. Witt's will to conquer makes any sense to her. 'Every continent', Lawrence says about the spirit of place, 'has its own great spirit of place. Every person is polarized in some particular locality, which is home, the homeland' (*SCAL* 5–6). In her homeland at last, Lou finds the great spirit which 'soothes' her and 'holds' her up and sometimes 'hurt(s)' and 'wear(s)' her down: it is 'something big, bigger than men, bigger than people, bigger than religion' (*StM* 155). Lou's perception of 'a bristling, almost demonish guardian' when she sees the pine tree is probably based upon Lawrence's own experience in New Mexico. He was deeply impressed by a sense of Pan in a pine tree where his ranch was:

It is a great tree, under which the house is built. And the tree is
still within the allness of Pan (…) It vibrates its presence into
my soul, and I am with Pan. I think no man could live near
a pine tree and remain quite suave and supple and compli-
ant. Something fierce and bristling is communicated. ('Pan in
America', *MM* 158)

Lou's life at the ranch seems like that of a priestess for she wants to serve the
spirit of the American soil in the secluded place, abandoning worldly values.
She is purely religious, searching for the sacred life. Her worship of Pan
and the wild spirit is not Christian. Her blood responds not to Christianity
but to 'the religious systems of the pagan world' which, Lawrence says in
Studies in Classic American Literature, 'did what Christianity has never
tried to do: they gave the true correspondence between the material cosmos
and the human soul' ('First Version 1918–19'; *SCAL* 260). Lou's blood
truly corresponds with 'the material cosmos'. She will be transformed
into a priestess whose blood also beats with 'the material cosmos' in *The
Escaped Cock.*

iii

There is another religious seeker in Lawrence's American fiction: Ramon
in *The Plumed Serpent.* Lou decides to live alone in a ranch like a priestess, giving up her social life yet awaiting a new 'bigger and stronger and
deeper' man (*StM* 154). Ramon is, on the other hand, not only a priest but
also a social reformer as leader of the Quetzalcoatl revival movement.
He wants to create a new society by restoring the traditional religion
of Mexico. He believes that the religion of Quetzalcoatl and other gods
should replace the Catholic Church, because the church in Mexico has lost
its living power. Though his religion seems pagan it is not quite so. His
teaching of the Quetzalcoatl cosmology is tinged with Christian terminology, whether it is from the Bible or from Congregational hymns. As John
Worthen points out:

'I am the Morning and the Evening Star,' says Ramon: 'Jesus
says I am the root and offspring of David, and the bright and
morning star.' (…) The repeated refrain 'Quetzalcoatl has

come!' draws on the refrain 'Deliverance will come!' – in the last verse, 'Deliverance has come!' – from the hymn 'I saw a way-torn traveller'. (*StM* 161)

This means that since Ramon is 'almost pure Spaniard' (*PS* 64) his spiritual backbone as westerner has been formed under the influence of Christianity, however hard he might try to replace the church with a pagan cosmology. Since the novel does not tell us where Ramon learned Congregational hymns, the closeness of Ramon's song to the Congregational hymn (such as John Worthen indicates) would be attributed to Lawrence himself because – as he says in 'Hymns in a Man's Life' – he loved Congregational hymns so much as a child that they were 'woven so deep in me' (*LEA* 130) and they are 'the same to my man's experience as they were to me nearly 40 years ago' (*LEA* 131). In other words Lawrence cannot create Ramon of western blood as spiritual leader without relying upon his own Christian background – hence the Quetzalcoatl religion with the Christian traits.

The Quetzalcoatl revival movement in *The Plumed Serpent* spreads gradually among the Mexican Indians because Quetzalcoatl and the other gods are deities of their own land who appeal to their blood consciousness. To Kate Leslie, a western woman, the appeal is ambiguous. She, being of Celtic blood, is attracted to the Quetzalcoatl movement because it gives her a powerful sense of the cosmic life she lacks (but at the same time she feels repelled because the pagan deities and rituals are entirely non-European so that her blood consciousness cannot fully accept them). Ramon and his trusted man Cipriano, another leader of the movement, were 'no doubt right for themselves, for their people and their country. But for herself ultimately, ultimately she belonged elsewhere' (*LEA* 387). For this reason, when she marries Cipriano – who is of 'pure Indian' blood (*LEA* 64) – and begins a new life with him in Mexico, she does not tell him in a positive tone about her decision to stay but says only: 'You won't let me go!' (*LEA* 444).

Kate's reservations seem to reflect Lawrence's attitude toward traditional Mexican religion. As a European, he cannot totally commit himself to it, even if the Mexican experience almost 'shattered' his Christian cultural background; as he says in *Mornings in Mexico*:

> The Indian way of consciousness is different from and fatal to our way of consciousness. Our way of consciousness is different from and fatal to the Indian's. The two ways, the two streams are never to be united. They are not even to be reconciled. There is no bridge, no canal of connection. (*MM* 61)

Therefore, for his European readers, Lawrence must find a way of attaining such a cosmic life as the Mexicans have within a framework of European cultural tradition. European readers cannot be Ramons or Ciprianos: Ramon's philosophy of life is valid only in Mexico. Compared with the Indian background of *The Plumed Serpent* a short story called 'The Overtone' (which was written in 1924 while Lawrence was working on the novel) provides a more convincing answer for European readers: Elsa Laskell, an English girl, tells us that she is 'a Pan's nymph' in the darkness and 'a Christian' in the pale light in England ('The Overtone', *StM* 16).

Before *The Plumed Serpent* Lawrence wrote *Kangaroo*, in which Somers (like Kate in *The Plumed Serpent*) cannot be at home with the aboriginal spirit. While he is in Cornwall, 'a country that makes a man psychic' (*K* 226), Somers feels as if the Celtic deities (the Tuatha de Danaan) will come:

> He would go out into the blackness of night and listen to the blackness, and call, call softly, for the spirits, the presences he felt coming downhill from the moors in the night. 'Tuatha de Danaan!' he would call softly. 'Tuatha de Danaan! Be with me. Be with me.' And it was as if he felt them come. (*K* 226)

But in Australia he cannot feel comfortable with its spirit of place, because he feels threatened by the evil spirit of the bush. Like Quetzalcoatl the spirit is of non-European origin, and Somers cannot be happy with it.

Just as Rico in *St. Mawr* cannot see Pan in the horse, neither can Clifford in *Lady Chatterley's Lover* see Pan in the forest. For Clifford the forest is what he conquers according to his will: he cannot feel beauty or compassion for natural things. Mellors, like Lewis in *St. Mawr,* is a man in whom Pan dwells. Just as Lewis's body 'seems to sink' (*StM* 38) in the horse which is 'Pan' (*StM* 66), Mellors is at one with the inner life of the forest: he is with 'the spirit of the wood' (*LCL* 20). His life in the forest makes him believe in the existence of 'the great god Pan'. For Mellors, the forest represents the world of sacred life exemplified by Pan, which is quite contrary to Clifford's mechanical world. When she flees from her husband's lifeless world to the forest to find solace, Connie significantly feels it to be a 'sanctuary' (*LCL* 20). The word suggests the existence of a deity, which is 'the spirit of the wood', or 'Pan'. As the forest gradually revives Connie's weakened physique and soul, her life begins to root itself in the world of Pan where Mellors lives, and the forest becomes the sacred life source for them both. Upon this source their relationship is built. When she unexpectedly calls at his cottage, Connie sees Mellors washing himself 'with a queer, quick little motion', 'quick, subtle as a weasel playing with water' (*LCL* 66) and is taken by surprise. The weasel image suggests that Mellors is a creature of the forest and has animal-like power. Connie is fascinated by his 'warm white flame of a single life revealing itself in contours that one might touch' (*LCL* 66), and her physical sense is awakened.

Later Connie has sexual intercourse with Mellors in the hut, 'the supernatural centre' as Squires calls it (*LCL* 207), and she is physically revived. Mellors has abandoned his social self, preferring to live alone in the forest, but now he begins to live as a social individual with Connie in 'tenderness', which is another form of love and a Christian virtue, and Connie is led to share it. For Mellors, tenderness entails not only spiritual but also physical awareness, which Christianity has long disregarded. Mellors hopes through tenderness to make whole the over-spiritualized Christian ethic of love and marriage. His relationship with Connie develops to fulfilment and wholeness both in the spiritual and the physical sense. Therefore, on the one hand, their marriage is such an embodiment of the 'old pagan vision' as Dennis Jackson argues, (because they are deeply rooted in the forest life) but on the other hand their marriage is based upon the Christian virtue because they are going to live in tenderness (though they are not regarded as Christian in the traditional sense). Besides, since they are sexually united in 'the supernatural centre' in the forest their marriage is – as it were – sanctified there. As Lawrence says in 'A Propos of *Lady Chatterley's Lover*' marriage as sacrament is

'Christianity's great contribution to the life of man' (*LCL* 322) and their marriage is placed in this Christian tradition, too.[1] Hence the modified or revitalized Christian ethic of love and marriage or, as Mark Spilka remarks, the 'paganization or transvaluation of current Christian belief' (213).[2]

Since physical awareness is of nature as well as of the body the physical selves of Connie and Mellors are closely connected with nature, and the body and nature should be regarded as interrelated – not separate – entities. Originally, Connie likes 'the *inwardness* of the remnant of forest' (*LCL* 65) (Lawrence's italics) and feels throbbing life in the forest before she comes to know Mellors:

> (she) sat down with her back to a young pine-tree, that swayed against her with curious life, elastic and powerful rising up (…) And she watched the daffodils go sunny, in a burst of sun, that was warm on her hands and lap. (*LCL* 86)

And, as the love between Connie and Mellors grows, the life of the surrounding forest penetrates into her more powerfully. For instance, after she is newly born as 'a woman' and filled with 'mystery' (*LCL* 174–75) through intercourse with Mellors, she feels the trees and earth alive:

> As she ran home in the twilight, the world seemed a dream; the trees in the park seemed bulging and surging at anchor on a tide, and the heave of the slope to the house was alive.(*LCL* 178)

Mellors awakens Connie's sense of life-mystery: the trees and earth quicken her, too. The trees and earth are in vital connection with her. Her relation with the trees and earth would be Celtic, because the Celts worshipped trees and the earth and nature in general, and Connie is of Scottish blood: her father was 'the burly Scottish knight' and she herself 'a bonny Scotch trout' (*LCL* 18). Connie's Celtic background, thus, easily enables her to become a living part of the forest where Mellors lives. The sharp sense of its life-mystery is a common feature between the Connie of Celtic blood and the Pan-like Mellors.

The harmony between their bodies and natures signifies the harmony between humanity and nature which Clifford completely lacks, being obsessed with a will to conquer. Connie and Mellors (by achieving a harmonious relationship between themselves and with nature) stand in complete opposition to Clifford and the marriage between Connie and Mellors is, as we have said, in the Christian tradition. Therefore, the vital connection with nature – which is pagan – works together with it to take the place of Clifford's mechanical and lifeless world.

The hut as 'the supernatural centre' of *Lady Chatterley's Lover* becomes the temple of Isis, also situated in a forest, in *The Escaped Cock*. The man who died comes to the temple where he and the priestess are sexually united, and he is given a new life. So far, the spiritual has suppressed the sensual within the stranger's psyche for, as saviour-teacher, he had unknowingly asked people to serve him 'with the corpse of their love', that is, with bodiless love, not with 'the soft warm love which is in touch' (*EC* 594). His contact with the pagan priestess now releases his sensual urge and thus the balance is established between the spiritual and the sensual, or between the Christian and the pagan. The cock which the stranger has released from the peasant's hands symbolizes both his now-released sensual urge as well as that of the Christians in general.

The priestess is searching for Osiris, whose role the stranger plays in their sexual union in the temple. In Egyptian mythology Osiris is not only the male god of the fructification of the land but also a symbol of the human soul, which is fettered by superficially attractive yet lifeless knowledge, for in the myth he is deceived by his cunning brother Set and places himself in a decorated coffin designed by him. He is shut in and killed and thrown into the river Nile. Isis, goddess of procreation and birth, finds her dead husband's body and revives him and brings him back into vital contact with the cosmos (Ohnuma 32–3). In *The Escaped Cock* the stranger, like Osiris, is fettered by the principle of bodiless love (from which he is released by the priestess of Isis and is thus made sensually alive). He realizes that man and woman are part of the greater cosmic life or 'the great rose of Space':

(…) the man looked at the vivid stars before dawn, as they rained down to the sea, and the dog-star green towards the sea's rim. And he thought: How plastic it is, how full of curves and folds like an invisible rose of dark-petalled openness, that shows where dew touches its darkness! How full it is, and great beyond all gods. How it leans around me, and I am part of it, the great rose of Space. I am like a grain of its perfume, and the woman is a grain of its beauty. Now the world is one flower of many-petalled darknesses, and I am in its perfume as in a touch. (*EC* 160)

Just as Connie's rebirth through contact with Mellors as Pan-believer sounds both pagan and Christian, so does the stranger's through contact with the priestess as Isis-devotee. Since the man who died no doubt suggests Christ and therefore symbolizes Christianity the man's rebirth is also that of Christianity, through the contact with the great life of 'the material cosmos' of which Isis and Osiris are part. *The Escaped Cock* is Lawrence's final achievement in the reconciliation of Christianity with paganism.[3] In addition, in this novella there is another god besides Isis and Osiris: 'the all-tolerant Pan' as a guardian of slaves 'with their ruddy broad hams and the small black heads' (*EC* 151). Isis, Osiris and Pan are all suggestive of the procreative and generative power of nature.

iv

Lawrence's characters are best able to respond to deities of European origin like Pan, the dryads, the spirit of England and the Tuatha de Danaan or to more exotic deities like Isis or Osiris, with which they are familiar. To Lawrence and to European readers of his fiction those of non-European origin like Quetzalcoatl or the spirit of the Australian bush would not appeal to their blood consciousness, because the non-European way of consciousness is different from the European way.

In the unconsciousness of Europeans there slumber many pagan deities of their past: Celtic, Germanic, Greco-Roman and Egyptian. The Catholic Church at first reconciled Christianity with pagan rituals. According to Lawrence in 'A Propos of *Lady Chatterley's Lover*' the Church (which knew that 'man doth not live by man alone, but by the sun and moon and earth in their revolutions') (*LCL* 328) established the Christian calendar upon the basis of the pagan life cycle so that man could live in rhythm with the cosmos. Lawrence seeks to return to traditional Christian thinking in *Lady Chatterley's Lover* and *The Escaped Cock* when trying to reconcile Christianity with paganism in his later fiction.

Lawrence believes that a clue for the recovery of vitality is found among the ancient peoples who, having had a closer touch with their circumambient universe, saw gods everywhere and in everything:

> To the ancient consciousness, Matter, Materia, or Substantial things are God. A great rock is God. A pool of water is God. And why not? The longer we live the more we return to the oldest of all visions. A great rock is God. I can touch it. It is undeniable. It is God. Then those things that move are doubly God. That is, we are doubly aware of their godhead: that which is, and that which moves: twice godly. Everything is a 'thing', and every 'thing' acts and has effect: the universe is a great complex activity of things existing and moving and having effect. And all this is God. (*A* 95)

The recovery of unity between man and nature is suggested in Annable, Lou, Mellors and the priestess, all of whom consciously or unconsciously serve Pan or Isis in nature. It was, indeed, 'a Herculean undertaking'[4] (as Keith Sagar points out) to uphold the Pan principle as a source of vitality in Lawrence's time, for nature was disappearing under the threat of industrialism. By the incorporation of a cosmic life sense and nature deities in his works, Lawrence also wanted to create a balance between Christianity and paganism. The vision of the balance is first suggested, though incompletely, in Annable in *The White Peacock* and finds its final expression in the last two fictional works: *Lady Chatterley's Lover* and *The Escaped Cock*.

Notes

1. For an echo of 'the Christian view' in *Lady Chatterley's Lover*, see Jarrett-Kerr, p. 103.
2. For this reason it is quite natural that Jarrett-Kerr declares that 'I do not want to claim Lawrence as any kind of a Christian' (23), whereas Spilka states that 'Lawrence is almost a Christian, after all' (217).

3. See also LeDoux's analysis of this novella in which he argues: 'Lawrence does not use the Christ myth to revitalize the Isis-Osiris myth (…) He is not attempting to return to paganism, but to return Christianity to its vital archetypal sources' (138).

4. Sagar, 'Introduction', *The Complete Short Novels*, ed. Keith Sagar and Melissa Partridge, p. 34.

CHAPTER 5

NATURE DEITIES: REAWAKENING BLOOD CONSCIOUSNESS IN THE EUROPEANS

i

In a letter of 8 December 1915 to Bertrand Russell Lawrence says that he became aware in his early twenties that there was blood consciousness as well as mental consciousness in the human psyche and that he became convinced of this belief when he read James G. Frazer's *The Golden Bough* and his *Totemism and Exogamy*. These two books taught him that primitive men with a belief in animism had profound blood consciousness. In the same letter he also attacks Russell by saying that his tragedy and the tragedy of modern people is that mental consciousness exerts its tyranny over blood consciousness (*L* ii 469–71). Lawrence believes that mental consciousness is one half of life and blood consciousness the other half and that one should not exclude the other. He regards Russell as a typical example of modern people who are obsessed with mental consciousness. For this reason Lawrence tries to restore a balance between mental consciousness and blood consciousness. He especially tries to awaken blood consciousness through his writings because it is disregarded by modern writers. Herein lies his unique approach to this serious modern problem. As Philipp Rieff points out, 'blood consciousness is nothing new in the English literary tradition; Shakespeare had it (…) What is new in Lawrence is his hymn-singing attitude towards the physicality of life' (53). One of the unique ways for him to quicken blood consciousness is to introduce nature deities or animistic perception in his works. In her book *From Persephone to Pan*, Viinikka discusses Lawrence's 'mythic elements' (25) in his works of the early 1920s. But Lawrence's mythic elements are found not only in these works but also in the works of the late 1920s and even before the 1920s.

I will first discuss the way Lawrence treats nature deities or animistic perception to vitalise blood consciousness in his works. Then I will take up Rieff's idea of the mythmaker as therapist and show how it applies to the European's need for blood consciousness. Finally, this chapter will demonstrate that blood consciousness is evident not only in Lawrence's works of the early 1920s but also before and after those years.

ii

In late December 1915 Lawrence moved from Hampstead Heath to Cornwall, where he perceived a Celtic consciousness. In January 1916 he wrote to Russell again:

> Cornwall isn't England. It isn't really England nor Christendom. It has another quality: of King Arthur's days, that flicker of Celtic consciousness before it was swamped under Norman and Teutonic waves. I like it very much. I like the people also. They've got a curious softness, and intimacy. I think they've lived from just the opposite principle to Christianity: self-fulfilment and social destruction, instead of social love and self sacrifice. (*L* ii 505)

The Celtic consciousness appeals not only to English but also to other European readers because it is of continental origin.

Lawrence's intimacy with the Cornish people and the Celtic consciousness is later reflected in the 1923 novel *Kangaroo*. In *Kangaroo* Somers spends a few months during the war in Cornwall before he is forced to leave by the police, who suspect him and his German wife (Harriet) of being German spies. In this novel Lawrence says that Cornwall, which is full of 'savage vibrations' (*K* 238), makes people 'psychic' (*K* 226) and when Somers walks out at night he feels as if the Celtic deities (the Tuatha de Danaan) were about to come (*K* 226).

The spirit of Celtic places in Cornwall awakens Somers's blood consciousness more deeply in autumn when he helps his friend, the Cornish farmer John Thomas, with the corn harvest: sitting on the sheaves Somers feels as though he were in the world of the Celts:

> And as Somers sat there on the sheaves in the underdark, seeing the light swim above the sea, he felt he was over the border, in another world. Over the border, in that twilit, awesome world of the previous Celts. The spirit of the ancient, pre-christian world, which lingers still in the truly Celtic places, he could feel it invade him in the savage dusk, making him savage too, and at the same time, strangely sensitive and subtle, under-standing the mystery of blood-sacrifice (...) (*K* 237)

And Somers loves to drift 'back into the blood-sacrificial pre-world, and the sun-mystery, and the moon-power, and the mistletoe on the tree away from his own white world, his own machine-conscious day. Away from the burden of intensive mental consciousness' (*K* 238). Though his blood-knowledge is deeply awakened in Cornwall he and his wife are suddenly ordered by the police to leave. This departure corresponds with the Lawrences', which was ordered in 1917.

In 1916 *Twilight in Italy* was published. Lawrence and Frieda had made an adventurous walk to Italy in 1912 after their elopement to Germany, and he observed many Italians who were essentially sensuous and 'pagan'. Like the Cornish, they had rich blood consciousness. Lawrence met one of the most typical Italians, called Il Duro, of whom Lawrence says, 'sensation itself was absolute – not spiritual consummation, but physical sensation (...) He belonged to the god Pan, to the absolute of the senses' (*TI* 177–8). But Il Duro, though he was a man of physical sensation, could not be an ideal man for Lawrence because this Italian lacked another important human value: spiritual consummation, which was not balanced with physical sensation. Therefore Lawrence can only praise Il Duro's Pan-power as such and no more.

In 1919, three years after the publication of *Twilight in Italy*, Lawrence returned to Italy. During his stay in Taormina, Sicily, he wrote his famous poem 'Snake', in which a snake is felt to be a god. Although he repeatedly criticizes modern people for relying too much upon mental consciousness and destroying blood consciousness and spontaneous life he is himself this sort of modern person, as he confesses in this poem. The poet is divided between mental consciousness and blood consciousness when he sees a snake come to drink at his water trough. First, he hears the voice of his education (that is, his mental consciousness) saying that it must be killed for it is venomous. But a few moments later he says he likes the snake, who has come 'like a guest' from the world of darkness. Besides, he feels so 'honoured' to have this guest that he dares not kill it instantly:

> Was it cowardice, that I dared not kill him?
> Was it perversity, that I longed to talk to him?
> Was it humility, to feel so honoured?
> I felt so honoured. (*Poems* 304)

The snake even looks 'like a god'. Yet, being overcome by the repeated voice of his education, he throws a stick at him to 'finish him off' (which does not hit him, though). When the god-like snake disappears into the hole from which he has come the poet misses him very much:

> And I wished he would come back, my snake.
>
> For he seemed to me again like a king,
> Like a king in exile, uncrowned in the underworld,
> Now due to be crowned again.
>
> And so, I missed my chance with one of the lords
> Of life. (*Poems* 305)

'One of the lords / Of life' is, in other words, a god of life coming from the underworld. Here Lawrence's animistic perception is evident. It is what his mental consciousness first tried to suppress, but what he is finally forced to recognize. It is an antithesis to the white consciousness of the European civilisation, which has been – as Lawrence says in *Apocalypse*, posthumously published in 1931 – an 'ideal civilisation' (*A* 78) for two thousand years and has been neglecting blood consciousness. The fatal blow which the ideal civilisation gave to Europe was the first world war, which Lawrence says, 'finished me' and 'was the spear through the side of all sorrows and hopes' (*L* ii 268). Not only 'Snake' but also *Birds, Beasts and Flowers* in its entirety expresses Lawrence's wish to restore that blood consciousness which has long been lost, so that European readers might be made vitally alive again. In this book, which came out in 1923, the world of animals and plants offers more chances for quickening and renewal than does the human world.

When Lawrence went to the Black Forest in Germany in 1921 his blood consciousness was sharply awakened, without being inhibited by any voice of his education. In that year he stayed in Baden-Baden for two months and began to write *Fantasia of the Unconscious,* sitting against a tree in the forest. In this book he makes an interesting digression about the trees while he expounds his theory on the planes and plexuses of a baby: in the forest he is strongly impressed by the power of tree life:

> The trees seem so much bigger than me, so much stronger in life, prowling silent around. I seem to feel them moving and thinking and prowling, and they overwhelm me. Ah well, the only thing is to give way to them. (*FU* 85)

When he feels 'the powerful sap-scented blood roaring up the great columns' of the magnificent trees, he comes to understand tree worship:

> I come so well to understand tree worship. All the old Aryans worshipped the tree. My ancestors. The tree of Life. The tree of knowledge. Well, one is bound to sprout out some time or other, chip off the old Aryan block. I can so well understand tree worship. And fear the deepest motive. (*FU* 86)

Here Lawrence does not use the word 'deity'. Yet it is certain that he presupposes a deity, probably Pan, when he says that he worships the tree.

He retained the same intuition when he went to America in 1922. In the previous year he was invited to come to America by Mabel Dodge Sterne, an American lady who later married an Indian (Tony Luhan). In America Lawrence lived in New Mexico, in a cabin on Lobo (later he calls it Kiowa) Ranch, in front of which 'a big pine tree rises like a guardian spirit' as he writes in an essay called 'Pan in America' in 1924:

The tree has its own aura of life. And in winter the snow slips off it, and in June it sprinkles down its little catkin-like pollen tips, and it hisses in the wind, and it makes a silence within a silence. It is a great tree (…) And the tree is still within the allness of Pan. (*MM* 158)

This is Lawrence's explicit Pan worship (which was firmly established around the early 1920s) although his Pan attachment or belief had already been expressed in *Twilight in Italy,* as we have seen, and in his novel of 1911 – *The White Peacock* – where Annable appears as Pan, and in a book review in 1913 (to which we shall refer later).

Another example of Pan worship in the American period is found in *St. Mawr*, which was finished on Lobo Ranch in 1924 (Sagar, *Calendar* 138). In this novella Lou Carrington (an American lady), while still in England leading a superficial life in upper-class society, comes to worship the horse named St. Mawr as Pan when she is overwhelmed by the 'mysterious fire of the horse's body'. She feels as if the horse was coming 'out of the everlasting darkness' 'like a god':

Almost like a god looking at her terribly out of the everlasting darkness, she had felt the eyes of that horse; great, glowing, fearsome eyes, arched with a question, and containing a white of light like a threat. What was his non-human question, and his uncanny threat? She didn't know. He was some splendid demon, and she must worship him. (*StM* 31)

Lou feels threatened and challenged by the horse to throw away her ordinary commonplace self and is led to a new dimension of life which is never shown by her aristocratic husband, Sir Henry Carrington.

While Lawrence was in New Mexico he made journeys to Mexico and wrote a Mexican novel called *The Plumed Serpent* in which Ramon, leader of a movement to revive the traditional Mexican Indian religion, wants to bring back the ancient gods Quetzalcoatl and Huitzilopochtli. Through the mouth of Ramon, who wants Mexican people 'to learn the name of Quetzalcoatl' and 'to speak with the tongues of their own blood', Lawrence wishes that each race would revive its own gods:

> I wish the Teutonic world would once more think in terms of Thor and Wotan and the tree Igdrasil. And I wish the Druidic world would see, honestly, that in the mistletoe is their mystery, and that they themselves are the Tuatha de Danaan, alive, but submerged. And a new Hermes should come back to the Mediterranean, and a new Ashtaroth to Tunis; and Mithras again to Persia, and Brahma unbroken to India, and the oldest dragons to China. (*PS* 248)

The same motif is taken up again in a poem called 'All sorts of gods' in *Last Poems,* published posthumously in 1932, in which Lawrence says that all sorts of gods and goddesses of all races are seen 'alive and moving' even today (*Poems* 579). This poem (as well as Ramon's speech on the gods) is a more developed and more emphatic illustration of Lawrence's early worship of all gods, which he expressed in a book review of *Georgian Poetry 1911–12* in 1913:

> I worship Christ, I worship Jehovah, I worship Pan, I worship Aphrodite. But I do not worship hands nailed or running with blood upon a cross, nor licentiousness, nor lust. I want them all, all the gods. They are all God. (*IR* 204)

In 1913 Lawrence was thinking about the European gods but in the late 1920s, when he wrote *The Plumed Serpent* and 'All sorts of gods', he set his belief in all the gods in an international context. He believed that not only European races but other races should revive their own gods because the more aware he was of the unique religion of the Indian race the more he thought about the religion of other races as well, who were culturally equal to the European ones. 'Lawrence's polytheism' allows, as James C. Cowan indicates in *D. H. Lawrence's American Journey*: 'multiple versions of deity, all representations in different cultures of the one unknown god of the unuttered name' (43). Lawrence's most shocking experience in New Mexico and Mexico was his encounter with the Indians' religious sense of life. As he confesses in an essay called 'New Mexico' ,written in 1928, the red Indians' cosmic or animistic religion almost 'shattered' (*MM* 176) his Christian outlook, because their blood consciousness was so profound.

In the 1927 essays *Mornings in Mexico* he shows that, while Mexican Indians danced, they had direct or non-verbal communications with 'the centre of the earth' which, Lawrence says, 'We (whites) never realise' (*MM* 64). 'New Mexico', *Mornings in Mexico* and *The Plumed Serpent* show Lawrence's sincere concern with the Indians' religion.

Yet, however strongly impressed he may be with their animistic religion, he realizes that 'the Indian way of consciousness is different from and fatal to our way of consciousness', that there is 'no bridge' between them and that it is dangerous to mix the two ways (*MM* 61). This awareness is also reflected in Kate Leslie in *The Plumed Serpent*. Although she is strongly attracted to the Indians' cosmic religion she finds herself in an ambivalent position between the Indian culture and her own European one. Finally she is led to realize that 'ultimately, she belongs elsewhere' (*PS* 387): that is, to Europe. This really echoes Lawrence's realization of his own identity as European around this period, for he writes to Catherine Carswell from Questa, New Mexico in 1922 that: 'Truly I prefer Europe. (...) I belong to Europe' (*L* iv 362). Or he writes to Knud Merrild from Chapala, Mexico, in 1923 that: 'I know I am European. So I may as well go back and try it once more' (*L* iv 463). Unlike Kate Leslie in *The Plumed Serpent* the woman in the short story called 'The Woman Who Rode Away' gives up her identity as white, and sacrifices herself to the Indian god when she flees from 'an invincible slavery' (*WWRA* 40) that her husband forces upon her. Her action, however, would not satisfy European readers because (as Keith Sagar suggests in *The Art of D. H. Lawrence* (148)), they cannot identify themselves with the Indians so easily as this woman.

If Lawrence as European cannot rely upon the Indian way he must, instead, incorporate his European way more clearly into his own writings. Since he believes that blood consciousness for the European will be vitalised not by the Indian but by the European way of perception he introduces, more intentionally, Mediterranean or Celtic deities into his novels, short stories or poems, especially after 1922. For example, *St. Mawr* (as we have seen), *Lady Chatterley's Lover* (1928), *The Escaped Cock* (1929), such short stories as 'The Overtone' and 'The Last Laugh' (both of which were written in 1924 (Sagar, *Calendar* 134–5)) and such poems as 'God is Born', 'Middle of the World' and 'Invocation to the

Moon', all of which were published in *Last Poems*. In *St. Mawr* and *Lady Chatterley's Lover* the god Pan plays (whether in the form of a horse or a gamekeeper) an important role in leading the heroine, Lou Carrington or Connie Chatterley, to her new life. Margot Norris argues that St. Mawr symbolizes 'the biocentric universe' (298); the same with the gamekeeper Mellors together with the forest with whose 'spirit' he lives (*LCL* 20). In both cases the heroines are led from 'the anthropocentric universe' (Norris 298) to 'the biocentric universe'. In *St. Mawr* Lawrence also introduces Celtic deities, which Lewis believes in (107–09) and 'a spirit of place' (also of Celtic origin) which calls on Lou when she finds a ranch in America (155). In 'The Overtone' 'Pan and Christ' (*StM* 16) are equally respected by a young girl – Elsa Laskell – in whom Lawrence tries to balance blood consciousness and mental consciousness. When Lawrence establishes Pan-power in man he usually puts it in balance with mental or spiritual consciousness – in this case with Elsa's worship of Christ. In 'The Last Laugh' Pan is still alive in a bush in modern London, and his overwhelming power strikes a man to death or lames a man who denies him: Pan even threatens to ravage the church that denies him. When there was a great storm that blew out its windows and doors, Miss James says that '(a) leaf of the church Bible' blew right in her face and she saw Pan there (*WWRA* 135). In this story Pan is so predominant that there is no reconciliation between Pan worship and Christianity as in 'The Overtone'. In *The Escaped Cock* the priestess of Isis, an Egyptian goddess of fertility, revives through physical contact the Christ-like man who died (and he realizes that the cosmic life is greater than the human life): 'I am part of it, the great rose of space' (*EC* 160). The encounter between the man who died and the priestess suggests that the Christian love-ideal which became barren because of its excessive spirituality will be revived through contact with the Mediterranean pagan cosmic life principle.

In the above-mentioned three poems ancient Greek deities are evoked and, thus, Lawrence tries to transmit powerful life-awareness to his readers. In 'God is Born' he explains how a god is born in the struggle of becoming:

The history of the cosmos
is the history of the struggle of becoming.
When the dim flux of unformed life
struggled, convulsed back and forth upon itself, and broke at last into
    light and dark
came into existence as light,
came into existence as cold shadow
then every atom of the cosmos trembled with delight.
Behold, God is born!
He is bright light!
He is pitch dark and cold! (*Poems* 589)

Here 'God' is not the God of Christianity but a god in the pagan sense. In the pagan mind everything becomes a god when it strikes you, as when Lawrence discusses the birth of ancient Greek gods or *theoi* in *Apocalypse*:

> At the moment, whatever struck you was god. If it was a pool
> of water, the very watery pool might strike you: then that was
> god; or the blue gleam might suddenly occupy your conscious-
> ness: then that was god; or a faint vapour at evening rising
> might catch the imagination: then that was theos (...) (*A* 95)

Ancient people felt these ancient Greek gods and so do modern people now, as is suggested in 'All sorts of gods'. Therefore, as Lawrence says in 'Middle of the World', 'the Minoan gods' or 'the gods of Tiryns' are still felt in the Mediterranean:

> And the Minoan gods, and the gods of Tiryns
> are heard softly laughing and chatting, as ever;
> and Dionysos, young, and a stranger
> leans listening on the gate, in all respect. (*Poems* 602)

And in 'Invocation to the Moon', we can feel Lawrence's vivid sense of the moon as life-giver, when he invokes the lady of the moon or moon goddess:

Now, lady of the Moon, now open the gate of your silvery house

… … …

and set me again on moon-remembering feet
a healed, whole man, O Moon! (*Poems* 609)

iii

Why does Lawrence try to make us aware of these deities? Because he
thinks that 'with the coming of Socrates and the "spirit" (that is, the ideal
mind) the cosmos died. For two thousand years man has been living in
a dead or dying cosmos, hoping for a heaven hereafter' (*A* 96), and he
believes, therefore, that 'now we have to get back the cosmos' and 'the
great range of responses (to the cosmos) that have fallen dead in us have
to come to life again' (78). Lawrence wants to revive the cosmic sense
or blood consciousness more powerfully by introducing nature deities or
animistic perception into his works, because these deities have an even
more profound influence upon the human psyche than natural objects such
as the moon, the stars and the trees have. The restoration of the pagan or
animistic mind is not just a nostalgic return to the old but a sincere attempt
to restore that vital relationship between man and the cosmos that is now in
peril in modem Europe. Lawrence's animistic world really provides a vital
clue for 'human survival' (Gutierrez 50).

CHAPTER 6

THE WORLD OF ANIMISM IN CONTRAST WITH CHRISTIANITY IN *ST. MAWR*

i

The title of *St. Mawr* (1925) seems to be a misleading one, firstly because the horse St. Mawr disappears in the latter half of the story and secondly because the latter half deals not with St. Mawr but the American desert. The first half emphasizes St. Mawr as Pan and the second half emphasizes the desert as a spirit of place. Since Pan is a Greco-Roman god of life and the spirit of place is a Celtic deity the novella leads us to realize the existence of both the Greco-Roman deity and the Celtic one. In between the reader is also led to Lewis's speech on his belief in 'moon-people' (108) (that is, moon-fairies) and tree fairies (107), both of which are also Celtic. *St. Mawr* thus presents the world of pagan deities or animism from the beginning to the end, and itself has its own coherent world of paganism or animism, which is placed in the story as an opposite world view to Christianity. The animistic world in the first half (which is seen in the horse) corresponds with that in the second half (which is seen in the American desert), hence the animistic consistency. The animistic world throughout the novella is characterized by two contrastive aspects of nature: creative and destructive.

On *St. Mawr*, however, Eliseo Vivas (151–2) and Anne Darlington Barker (79) state that there is no consistency between the first half of the novella – where St. Mawr dominates as Pan – and the latter half, where the spirit of place is newly introduced. But both critics miss the point of pagan or animistic coherence and the significance of animism in the novella. In this chapter, firstly – by looking at key figures in the novella – I would like to demonstrate the animistic consistency and, secondly, I will also confirm that the pagan deity perception which has been belittled or neglected by Christianity is of universal value. The key figures in the story are Lou, Lewis, Rico, Mrs Witt, the Dean Vyner and the New England woman.

Lou and Lewis are endowed with animistic or ancient perception while Rico, Mrs Witt, the Dean Vyner and the New England woman represent the modern world or the world of Christianity. Lou and Lewis become or are aware of the animistic perception which Rico, Mrs Witt, Vyner and the New England woman have never known.

Lawrence's recovery of animism in *St. Mawr* in the 20th century – when considered in a European literary context – can be said to be a modern revival of the pagan spirit of the 19th-century German author Heinrich Heine, who tried to revive a pagan goddess Diana in his fiction *Die Göttin Diana* (*The Goddess Diana*) (1846). I will demonstrate, too, that just as *The Goddess Diana* is Heine's passionate attempt to restore pagan deity perception in 19th-century Germany, *St. Mawr* is Lawrence's attempt in 20th-century England.

ii

Lou Carrington leads a superficial life with her aristocratic husband Rico in London. She is suffering from inertia in her life because all her husband wants to do is to lead a pleasant social life in high society: he never intends to have a vivid fulfilment of life. His main concern in his life is to take pleasure and enjoy himself. As a fashionable man he also pays great attention to his outward appearance, which is indicated by his extraordinary obsession with clothes (Cowan, *Lawrence's American Journey* 82).

Therefore, though he is an artist, he cannot see the hidden mystery in things – for example, in St. Mawr – with 'the third eye' (*StM* 65), which is essential for an artist. He is, like Gerald Crich in *Women in Love* or Clifford Chatterley in *Lady Chatterley's Lover*, portrayed as a man who completely lacks this quality (along with the vitality of life).

When Lou, unlike Rico, sees the horse she is overpowered by the mysterious fire which she has never known, and she feels that it breaks her inner deadlock:

> But now, as if that mysterious fire of the horse's body had split some rock in her, she went home and hid herself in her room, and just cried. The wild, brilliant, alert head of St. Mawr seemed to look at her out of another world. It was as if she had had a vision, as if the walls of her own world had suddenly

melted away, leaving her in a great darkness, in the midst of which the large, brilliant eyes of that horse looked at her with demonish question, while his naked ears stood up like daggers from the naked lines of his inhuman head, and his great body glowed red with power. (…) He was some splendid demon, and she must worship him. (*StM* 30–1)

The 'mysterious fire' or 'demon' is later identified as 'Pan' (*StM* 66). Lou's dormant sense of life or her 'third eye' is thus awakened by the Pan-power of the horse, and her intuitive faculty therefore becomes keenest among all her associates (Rico, Mrs Witt, Cartwright, Mr and Mrs Vyner, the Manby girls and Frederick Edwards). To Lou (in the above scene) St. Mawr appears as a life-revealing or creative Pan but – to Rico or his friend Edwards – the horse shows itself as a destructive power, because they are very careless of St. Mawr as an awful animal. This contrast is quite in parallel with that in Heine's *The Goddess Diana,* where a German knight is shown vivid vitality by the goddess Diana and follows her while his wife – a superficial woman – cannot intuit it at all.

While Lou is attracted to St. Mawr and worships him as Pan, her husband and Frederick Edwards turn out to be enemies to the horse. When riding out to the Welsh border with Edwards and other people Rico is surprised at the sudden rearing up of the horse, and is nearly thrown off. He tries – in an instant – to force the horse under his rein, but in vain. He is struck down and lamed forever. He does not have any consideration of why the horse rears up so suddenly, and he has no compassionate feeling towards the horse. He is just domineering over the horse. In this scene the meaning of Rico's hidden will to subjugate the animal is revealed by the author: that is, the human is placed in a superior position over the animal as a conqueror. His will is, however, repudiated by St. Mawr or Pan-power in the end. So is the will of Edwards, who receives a hard kick from the horse's hoof on his face. Neither Rico nor Edwards has the third eye to see the Pan-power in St. Mawr: they just see the horse as an object with their physical eyes. They are those who boast of human superiority over the animal or nature itself. They are essentially cut off from nature. Against these men St. Mawr shows himself as a destructive force.

It is true that among the characters in the novella Cartwright and the

Dean Vyner talk about Pan in a conversation with Rico and his friends at a party. Yet Cartwright's talk is, as Mrs Witt points out (*StM* 67), limited to the surface level and he cannot intuit Pan: his intuitive faculty is dead. Cartwright, therefore, 'expounds and represents the wrong sort of Pan, the "fallen Pan"' (Merivale 203).

Vyner is also another fallen Pan. Although he talks of Pan he does not feel any Pan-power in anything, either. Therefore he easily proposes that the horse should be gelded after Rico's accident. His proposal betrays his idea of a man as a superior being over an animal. He pays attention to Rico the man, but not to St. Mawr the animal. And, though Vyner shows respect for Mrs Witt as a rich woman, he looks down on her as 'a parvenu American' (*StM* 43). His respect is only for 'riches' (*StM* 43), and this means that he is a complete materialist. He thinks only of man and his riches and it is thus shown that Vyner, dean as he is, is a narrow-minded and man-centred person. Here we can see Lawrence's criticism of Vyner's man-centred Christian idea and materialism.

Although Mrs Witt feels repugnant towards Vyner's materialism she shares his idea of man's superiority, too, because she is obsessed with the idea of conquest. She is so energetic an American woman and so much possessed with the will to conquer that she is driven to subjugate men under her. She even tries to conquer God: 'she had a terrible contempt for the God that was supposed to rule this universe. She felt she could make *him* kiss her hand' (*StM* 102) (Lawrence's italics). Having no fear of God, she glorifies herself as a conquering woman. Yet her self-glorification is undermined by the sense of emptiness, which gradually gnaws at her soul.

Mrs Witt's will to conquer is also a characteristic of the New England woman, who tries to conquer natural forces at her ranch. The New England woman – who believes in the love of almighty God – cannot see any evidence of the benevolent God in her ranch when it is savaged by natural forces, while she tries to conquer nature to keep up her ranch. Just as Mrs Witt is an embodiment of man-conquering will, the New England woman is an embodiment of nature-conquering will. However hard the New England woman may try to subjugate nature with her will, natural forces destroy her attempt and threaten her to admit her vain efforts. She sometimes ponders: 'There is no Almighty loving God. The God there is shaggy as the pine-trees, and horrible as the lightning' (*StM* 147). This is a destructive aspect of the American desert. Although the inner voices tell her: the existence of a powerful life-force acting in nature she does not accept her defeat. The fact is, however, that she is – in the end – forced to leave the ranch, because she finds herself unable to manage the ranch with her willpower. Here is another criticism of the rigid or dogmatized Christianity which excludes and ignores the power of nature. However much the New England woman may consider the love of God to be almighty in the American desert, there is another life principle working in nature: destructive natural forces which she cannot conquer.

When Lou goes back to America and sees the ranch in the desert, she shows a different sensibility towards it from that of the New England woman. Lou is glad to see it and her heart leaps:

> (...) it was the place Lou wanted. In an instant, her heart sprang to it. The instant the car stopped, and she saw the two cabins inside the rickety fence, the rather broken corral beyond, and behind all, tall, blue balsam pines, the round hills, the solid uprise of the mountain flank: and getting down, she looked across the purple and gold of the clearing, downwards at the ring of pine-trees standing so still, so crude and untameable, the motionless desert beyond the bristles of the pine crests, a thousand feet below: and beyond the desert, blue mountains, and far, far-off blue mountains in Arizona: *'This is the place'* she said to herself. (*StM* 140) (Lawrence's italics)

Unlike the New England woman Lou accepts the wild desert as it is: she has no such intention to conquer, like the New England woman has.

When Lou later visits the ranch with her mother her experience of natural life is further deepened. She finds a spirit of place there and surrenders herself to it. For the New England woman the ranch is an object to conquer or make her own use of, and she cannot find anything sacred or awful in nature. Whereas Lou finds a spirit of place – that is, a sacred life-force – in the ranch and hears the call of it and she says to her mother:

'There's something else for me, mother. There's something else even that loves me and wants me. I can't tell you what it is. It's a spirit. And it's here, on this ranch. (…) And it's something to do with me. It's a mission, if you like. I am imbecile enough for that! – But it's my mission to keep myself for the spirit that is wild, and had waited so long here: even waited for such as me.' (*StM* 155)

Lou's service to the spirit of place is like that of a priestess. To surrender herself to the spirit of place in this scene or to Pan in the previous case is what uniquely characterizes Lou and makes her essentially different from her mother or her husband, who has never surrendered to anything or anyone. Mrs Witt cannot surrender herself to Pan or spirit of place: she is so much possessed with a dominant will to conquer others that she cannot intuit a god to whom she devotes herself. It is the same with Rico, Vyner and the New England woman: they have found nothing to which they surrender themselves. Lou's discovery of – first – Pan in St. Mawr and, then, of the spirit of place at the ranch means that she has discovered the greater life than human life: that is, the cosmic life to which she surrenders herself. Therefore St. Mawr in the story functions only as a guide (as Alan Wilde suggests (329)) who leads Lou to this greater cosmic life in the desert, and it is natural and inevitable that in America St. Mawr's role becomes unimportant or that the horse is replaced by the desert. 'The biocentric universe', or the cosmo-centric universe, replaces 'the homo-centric universe' (Norris 298). The idea of cosmic life is more brilliantly and passionately described in other essays, like 'New Mexico' (written around the time when *St. Mawr* was written) and *Apocalypse*, the last essay.

When Lou first saw St. Mawr she found Pan and worshipped him. It can be said that in the encounter with St. Mawr she unconsciously felt herself to be like a priestess devoting herself to Pan: unconsciously, because she was not aware of the sense of 'mission' which she later had for the spirit of place. St. Mawr now seems to her a saint whom she worships. Unchristian as the title of the horse sounds it is a suitable one in the animistic sense, because her worship is intended not as a Christian feeling but as an animistic one. Lawrence's aim to use the name of St. Mawr is to give a blow to man-centred Christianity and to evaluate and restore the animistic sense. And when Lou comes to the American desert she again finds herself like a priestess. Like a priestess she worships the spirit of place. Her repeated and, therefore, deepened priestess-like feeling is what Englishmen, Americans or Christians have failed to acknowledge. Their best example is Mrs Witt, or the New England woman who has never surrendered herself to nature. Wherever Lou discovers a deity in nature she thus sanctifies it by her intuitive faculty. For modern people such as Rico, Mrs Witt, the Vyners, Cartwright, Edwards, the Manby girls and the New England woman nature is just a thing to see or conquer, and they cannot intuit any deity in it. Lou is the only person in the novella (except for Lewis) who can intuit something sacred in nature and, having respect for it, she recovers the sense of sacredness. Lou's position in *St. Mawr* is entirely opposite to that of the moderns, and she is quite close to 'the inaudible, silent world' (*StM* 104) of the two grooms, Lewis and Phoenix.

Of these two grooms Lewis is more unique and important than Phoenix, who will sell his sex-power in exchange for white women's money. Lewis, in whom the 'last blood' of 'the old savage England' still flows (*StM* 73), not only lives in 'the inaudible, silent world' but also retains that vivid intuitive understanding of deities which Phoenix lacks. Being a Welsh groom, Lewis feels the throbbing life of St. Mawr, and is in oneness with it. Furthermore, he perceives deities in nature: he says that there are 'moon-people' who cleanse the air with moonlight and tree fairies, who protect one if one asks them pardon for cutting down a tree. This is a beneficial, or creative, aspect of nature. However, if one cuts down a tree without asking pardon, he says, one will be hurt by tree-people at night. This is a destructive aspect of nature. 'Moon-people' or tree fairies are used in the Celtic sense in the text, and he has a Celtic life-awareness. In this respect Lewis and Lou have something in common: Lou's sense of the spirit of place is also – traditionally speaking – a Celtic one, for the Celts are said to have had a firm belief in spirits of place.

When Lewis tells Mrs Witt of his belief in 'moon-people' or tree fairies she cannot understand him, and says that his belief is just a superstition. For Mrs Witt nature is a thing to observe as an object, whereas for Lewis nature is a living being to respect or communicate with. One good example of Lewis's view of nature is that he respects, as we have seen above, 'moon-people' or tree fairies and lives in 'another world' (*StM* 104) from hers. His world is '(a) world dark and still, where language never ruffled the growing leaves' (*StM* 104). Mrs Witt cannot understand his world because she 'had lived so long, and so completely, in the visible, audible world' (*StM* 104). She lives only with an analytical mind to 'vivisect' (*StM* 44) the visible world. For Mrs Witt nature and man are different and separate things and incommunicable. For Lewis, however, nature and man are in oneness and their lives are interpenetrating and both to be respected. Thus, he is in oneness with St. Mawr. Lou's discovery of Pan and the spirit of place means that she approaches Lewis's world of animism, and she realizes that nature is a living being to be respected because deities dwell in it. Such moderns as Rico, Vyner and Mrs Witt have lost the intuitive understanding and the feeling of respect because they rely too much on the conquering will. Mrs Witt, who is characterized by conquering will, has no respect for men's bodies (as Lewis points out (*StM* 112)). That is why she is rejected by Lewis when she proposes to him. Neither has she any respect for nature nor animistic perception of life, an essential feeling without which man would not be united with nature.

In other words, if Lou returns to the unified world of man and nature she must intuit and respect deities in nature first: then, and then only, she will be led to the blessed unity of man and nature. Since the perception of deities is a pagan or an animistic sense, Lou's discovery of deities is a modern recovery of the pagan or animistic sense. Although this animistic sense is not a Christian one at all it is not to be discarded, because it has its own universal value: it enables one to go back to the universal and blessed state of oneness of man with nature. The world of St. *Mawr* is, therefore, to lead the reader of the modern age to the significant meaning of respecting nature and to the universal value of animistic sense of life. Lou and Lewis are forerunners of it, blaming and rejecting the man-centring Christian ideology which aims to suppress nature under man's will.

Lou and Lewis are qualified to hold their intuitive faculty because they are not entirely bound by the Christian idea of love or man-centred world view, which tends to be forceful upon an individual. The forceful idea inevitably kills spontaneous life-flow, as is most evidently seen in the Dean Vyner or Rico.

Christianity often places man over animal and justifies man's superiority as a conqueror of nature. This is typically seen in the Dean Vyner's attitude toward St. Mawr when he proposes gelding him. Although Vyner is a dean he does not have any impartial view to judge Rico's accident. St. Mawr was not an 'evil' animal (*StM* 81), but just reared up on seeing a dead snake lying in front of him. When Lou ponders over evil she thinks that it is Rico, not St. Mawr, who is responsible for St. Mawr's sudden rearing. The horse did not do anything wrong, for which it must suffer from the punishment of gelding. Yet, Vyner hastily regards St. Mawr as an enemy toward Rico – who was lamed – and proposes gelding. The Dean Vyner is a caricature of man-centring Christianity, and the rigidness of his Christian idea of love is suggested by the invalidity of Mrs Vyner.

The sterility of Christian ideology is also criticized by Lewis – who does not believe the 'chapel-folks' (*StM* 109) – especially his uncle and aunt, who brought him up: they derisively call his belief in 'moon-people' and tree fairies a 'heathen' idea (*StM* 110). His belief is, however, what he holds wholeheartedly. He lives purely in the animistic world, which the Christian uncle and aunt cannot understand.

However, Lewis is not an appropriate man for Lou because, unlike any Lawrentian hero, he is not much critical of the present degenerate world and therefore is not seeking the unknown world which she is looking for. She needs a different man who would be 'bigger and stronger and *deeper* than I am' (154) (Lawrence's italics), and yet such a man has not appeared to her.

iii

Thus, *St. Mawr* contrasts the lifeless Christianity or western world with the powerful animism or paganism, to which Lawrence gives more importance to recover the sacredness of nature. In this respect the world of *St. Mawr* is in parallel with that of *Birds, Beasts and Flowers* or his essay 'New Mexico'. Many of animal poems in this book of poems show Lawrence's sense of sacredness in animal life. In 'Snake', for example, there is a conflict between two voices as in *St. Mawr*: one voice tells the poet to worship the snake and the other voice to kill it. To worship the snake is an animistic feeling, yet to kill it means to rely on the will of conquering. The poet is torn between the two opposite feelings and, in the end, he regrets his action of killing 'one of the lords / Of life' (*Poems* 305) with a clumsy log, and cherishes the feeling of worshipping it. In this poem, as in *St. Mawr*, the animistic feeling takes an important role. In the essay 'New Mexico', too, the animistic world view of Indians is overwhelming:

> I think New Mexico was the greatest experience from the outside world that I have ever had. It certainly changed me for ever. Curious as it may sound, it was New Mexico that liberated me from the present era of civilisation, the great era of material and mechanical development. (*MM* 176)

And this experience almost 'shattered the essential Christianity' on which his 'character was established' (*MM* 176).

However, we have to be very cautious in labelling him as a writer of the animistic world because he is also much aware of Christianity – as is seen in other works – such as the poem 'St Matthew', the short story 'The Overtone', the last novella *The Escaped Cock* or the last novel *Lady Chatterley's Lover*.

While in 'Snake', as mentioned above, the snake is worshipped as a god, or 'one of the lords / Of life', in 'St Matthew', however, the so-called 'via positiva' and 'via negativa' towards God in Christianity are pursued by the poet himself. In 'The Overtone' the daytime world of Christ's way and the night-time world of the nymph's way are both aimed at by Elsa Laskell. In *The Escaped Cock* the Jesus-like man who died gets married to the Isis-devotee priestess and their marriage is based on tenderness, or the Christian love ethic. And in *Lady Chatterley's Lover* Connie and Mellors transform themselves into nymph-like or satyr-like figures in the forest where the spirit of wood dwells (and they achieve a marriage based on tenderness, too).

Lou Carrington's animistic characteristic in *St. Mawr* can be viewed in this connection, and Lawrence is very much aware of the significance of animistic perception and the Christian way of thinking, though the latter is less emphasized in this novella.

And finally, when we consider *St. Mawr* within a literary and historical context of Europe, Lawrence's recovery of animism in *St. Mawr* in the 20th century can be said to be a reverberation of the impassioned voice of the 19th-century German author Heinrich Heine. Nearly 90 years before Lawrence, Heine tried to revive a pagan goddess Diana in *The Goddess*

Diana. In this fiction a German knight, refusing the superficial world where he has been living, finds true vitality in the forest goddess Diana[1]. While Lawrence prefers Pan as a god of life, Heine prefers Diana as a goddess of the forest: both authors share the pagan deity perception. There is also a parallel in their thinking of pagan life-awareness and Christianity between Heine's *Zur Geschichte der Religion und Philosophie in Deutchland (For the History of the Religion and Philosophy of Germany)* (1834) and Lawrence's *Apocalypse*. Lawrence indicates that 'to the pagan' 'the cosmos was a very real thing. A man *lived* with the cosmos, and knew it greater than himself ', and that 'we have lost the cosmos' in the age of Christianity (*A* 76) (Lawrence's italics). In a similar way Heine emphasizes the significance of the universal value of pagan deity perception and points out, too, that the dominating power of Christianity has long suppressed pagan deities and pagan thinking in Europe[2]. Just as *The Goddess Diana* is Heine's attempt through the knight to revive the pagan life-awareness in 19th-century Germany, *St. Mawr* is Lawrence's attempt through Lou Carrington in 20th-century England and America. Lawrence's novella, however, sounds more modern and universal because it is placed in a wider and more international context than that of Heine.

Notes

1. See Heinrich Heine, 'Die Göttin Diana', trans. Yoko Nagura, *Doitsu Romanha Zenshu (The Collected Works of German Romantics)* vol. 16, 189–92; also cf. Yoko Nagura, *'On Die Göttin Diana'*, pp. 121–41.
2. See Heinrich Heine, *Zur Geschichte der Religion und Philosophie in Deutchland*, trans. Yoshifumi Mori, *Heine Sanbun Sakuhinshu (Heine's Prose Works)* vol. 4, pp. 28–9.

CHAPTER 7

ST. MAWR, THE ESCAPED COCK AND *CHILD OF THE WESTERN ISLES* : THE REVIVAL OF AN ANIMISTIC WORLD VIEW IN THE MODERN WORLD

i

D. H. Lawrence's *St. Mawr* and *The Escaped Cock* were published in 1925 and 1929 respectively and, in 1957, 27 years after Lawrence's death, Rosalie K. Fry's children's story *Child of the Western Isles* was published. Although Fry does not seem to have been influenced by Lawrence's works her work echoes Lawrence's animistic world view, which is described in his two novellas: we can indicate that both writers share the same tradition of European animism and that they both try to revive an animistic world view in their own ways in the modem world, where man-centred ideology or materialism nearly stifles the lively animistic sense of life. Their trials to recover that sense seem to be their re-evaluation of the animistic world view, which the modern age has long disregarded or suppressed, in exchange for homo-centricism or material prosperity. The purpose of this chapter is to demonstrate this thesis by comparing the two writers: this seems to have received little attention from critics so far.

ii

In *St. Mawr* Lou Carrington leads a superficial life with her aristocratic husband, Rico, feeling no fulfilment in her life. Yet one day – as we have seen in Chapter 6 – when she sees the horse named St. Mawr she is overwhelmed by him, and she worships him as Pan (30–1). Comparing St. Mawr's vitality with her husband's superficial way of life among the upper class Lou finds that Rico entirely lacks real life, and she finds the same situation with his upper-class friends. Finally, she rejects Rico's world of superficiality and takes up St. Mawr's world of vitality. For her St. Mawr, having the title of saint, is a special, sacred animal. He appears to her out of 'another world': that is, the animal world, the untold value of which she has never known. He is (as it were) a visitor from the animal world, coming to her with the new message of vital life. And later in the novella a similar message was given to her by the spirit of place when she goes back to America. At a ranch in the Arizona desert she finds the spirit of place calling to her and thinks that 'it was the place (she) wanted' (*StM* 140).

And she decides to live there, serving its spirit. Thus, St. Mawr as Pan and the American land as spirit of place lead Lou to real life-forces and let her revere them and establish a living relationship with them (or with nature). In the novella Lewis, her Welsh groom, also believes in tree fairies and moon-fairies. He explains to Mrs Witt about how moon-people or fairies make the air clean:

> 'You sit on the pillow where they (the moon-people) breathe, and you put a web across their mouth, so they can't breathe the fresh air that comes from the moon. So they go on breathing the same air again and again, and that makes them more and more stupefied. The sun gives out heat, but the moon gives out fresh air. That's what the moon-people do: they wash the air clean with moonlight.' (*StM* 108)

Or about tree fairies he says:

> 'They say that ash-trees don't like people. When the other people were most in the country – I mean like what they call fairies, that have all gone now – they liked ash-trees best. And you know the little green things with little small nuts in them, that come flying down from ash-trees – pigeons, we call them – they're the seeds – the other people used to catch them and eat them before they fell to the ground. And that made the people so they could hear trees living and feeling things.' (107–8)

In Lewis's world view, which sounds Celtic or Germanic, the ash-trees and the tree fairies have an equal status of life in this world as men do. Man is not considered to be a centre of the universe, but part of it. The heroine, Lou, is also led to a similar world view as the story develops. Therefore, the central philosophy of *St. Mawr* is that man is not the centre of the universe but that he lives side by side with the cosmos as part of it, as Margot Norris indicates (Norris 298). In other words the Cartesian worldview – 'cogito ergo sum' – is rejected, and the cosmo-centred worldview or animism is adopted instead: man is not the measure of creation but is part of the cosmos. The same idea echoes in Lawrence's poems, 'Fish' and 'Climb down, O lordly mind', in which man's egocentrism or absolutism of the human mind is severely criticized (*Poems* 289–94; 410–11).

In *St. Mawr* there is another different type of character: Rico and his upper-class English friends. Their world view is all man-centred, as is typically seen in their fierce hatred against St. Mawr and their will to geld the horse: and in America, too, there is the New England woman whose stubborn will to conquer nature with the fixed and dogmatic belief of almighty God is extremely homo-centric. Unlike them, Lou and Lewis stand within the opposite world view of believing and serving the life of the cosmos. When she feels Pan and the spirit of place her perception is Greco-Roman and Celtic and when Lewis, of Welsh blood, senses tree fairies and moon-fairies, his perception is also Celtic. Since Lewis is a more static figure in the novella, Lou represents European animism more dramatically than the Welsh groom.

Similarly, European animism is revived in *The Escaped Cock*. It can be considered to be a novella of the marriage between Christianity and animism or, to use James C. Cowan's words, of '"the trembling balance" between Christianity and the Osiris myth' (Cowan, 'Allusions' 184), because the man who died gets married to the Isis-devotee who is in search of Osiris. While the Isis-devotee stands for Egyptian animism the man who died represents Christianity, which is severely criticized in the novella: Lawrence makes the man who died 'ponder on the bodilessness and lifelessness of his love', preaching (in other words) the rigid Christian doctrine:

> Suddenly it dawned on him: I asked them all to serve me with the corpse of their love. And in the end I offered them only the corpse of my love. This is my body – take and eat – My corpse –
>
> A vivid shame went through him. – After all, he thought, I wanted them to love with dead bodies. If I had kissed Judas with live love, perhaps he would never have kissed me with

> death. Perhaps he loved me in the flesh, and I willed that he
> should love me bodilessly, with the corpse of love. (*EC* 157–8)

Traditionally Christianity emphasizes spirituality too much and thus disregards man's physicality or the vivid contact with nature which (the man who died comes to believe) is to be balanced with spirituality. This balance is recovered when he gets married to the Isis-devotee. In other words the Egyptian animistic life principle 'revitalize(s)' (Cowan, 'Allusions' 174) the man who died, and thus the 'creative balance' (Cowan 185) between the two life principles is established. The Isis-devotee is depicted as part of the cosmos, serving Isis – goddess of vegetation – in a temple situated in a wood. The man who died is led to realize that 'I am part of the great Rose of space' (*EC* 160): that is, the great cosmos. He is thus led to share the same animistic world view as that of the Isis-devotee, establishing – with her aid – the living relationship with the cosmos which he had long disregarded.

In *Apocalypse* Lawrence accuses Christians of having escaped from the immediate contact with the cosmos and turned it into 'a mechanism of fate and destiny, a prison' (*A* 78) for two thousand years: 'Christianity and our ideal civilisation has been one long evasion' (*A* 78) of lively contact with the cosmos. He insists, therefore, that, if modern men get to be filled with vivid life, they recover with 'a sort of worship' (*A* 78) in their heart that contact with the cosmos which pre-Christian ancient people vividly possessed. When the man who died gets married to the Isis-devotee in *The Escaped Cock* he recovers the long-lost contact with the cosmos. *The Escaped Cock* and *Apocalypse* were written at the end of Lawrence's life and this novella as well as the last essay shows Lawrence's urgent and last appeal to Christians, who have long lost the cosmic life.

iii

A similar animistic world view found its way into Rosalie K. Fry's children's story, *Child of the Western Isles*, in 1957. Her work is based on the Welsh legend of a mermaid called 'The Lady of Llyn y Fan Fach', just as *St. Mawr* is partly based on a Celtic belief which is embodied in Lewis's belief of fairies. According to the Welsh legend a fisherman sees a beautiful lady on the beach. However, when she is seen by him, she suddenly disappears in the sea. She is a siren or a fairy. He cannot forget her and comes to the beach to see her again day after day. Finally, offering her the bread which was specially made with the advice of his mother, he asks the siren to become his wife. She consents to his proposal, on condition that if he strikes her three times in their marital life she will leave him forever. After they get married they have three children and he strikes her twice, forgetting his promise to her not to do so. Then, when she laughs during a funeral service, he strikes her for the third time (to warn her not to laugh) and again without realizing his promise. As he has broken his promise to her she instantly leaves him and her children and goes back to the sea. Since she cannot forget her children, however, she comes back one day to the eldest boy to teach him the art of healing so that he can serve his countrymen with this art. In the Llyn y Fan Fach legend the siren gives her husband children and teaches the children medical knowledge. The siren (who is endowed with a human soul) is treated equally as a human being, and the religious background of this legend is pure Celtic animism. (This legend is also used in Fry's other novel, *Whistler in the Mist,* whose setting is the Black Mountain with the Van Pool nearby in Wales. In this story the heroine Rosemary and her Aunt Betony are said to be descendants of the siren and Aunt Betony is a specialist of herbal medicine which, in the story, is a skill which has been handed down from the three sons of the siren).

Like in Lawrence's *St. Mawr* and *The Escaped Cock* European animism is obvious in Fry's *Child of the Western Isles,* too. As the grandfather of the heroine Fiona McConville tells her, all his family members are descendants of Mrs Ian McConville, a siren or fairy. One day Ian found a beautiful woman in Ron Mor Skerry or Isle and got married to her. From their marriage children were born and their offspring inherited the siren's blood generation after generation, together with the gifted skill of catching lots of fish. Their skill was what the seal-fairy had originally given her children, and fishery is their traditional profession protected by seals. While the 'seal-woman' teaches the eldest boy the art of healing in the legend, she gives her descendants the skill of catching fish (in Fry's story).

In Fry's story Celtic animism is contrasted with and set against modern materialism. Compared with Lawrence's severe criticism of modern man's materialism and egocentrism in *St. Mawr*, Fry's criticism in *Child of the Western Isles* is more soft-toned. Naturally, in the children's story, Fry makes an implicit criticism by saying that Fiona's family deserted Ron Mor

Isle (their homeland) in order to look for – as her grandfather comments – 'the rush and the noise of the cities' (17). Her father was not satisfied with a fisherman's simple life and decided to leave the island with his family to seek a new fortune: that is, material prosperity and success, in a city. He is an earnest aspirant for material success in an urban life, leaving the sea and abandoning the McConvilles' generations' long joy of 'learning the way of the wind when the tide is on the turn' (17). What he obtained as a factory worker in the city after he left the island was, however, a busy life and hard work – 'all day at the factory' (10) in the 'horrid' city, 'all grey and dirty, with people, people everywhere' (9). Living in the city Fiona herself suffers, falling victim to city life. She then is advised by a doctor to refresh herself in the old island where she spent her early years, and she goes back home. (Here again we notice another parallel between Fry's story and Lawrence's short story 'Sun' in which, following her doctor's advice, Juliet recuperates with lots of sunshine on her body on the island of Sicily in the Mediterranean sea after she falls ill in New York, a crowded modern city (*WWRA* 19–38)). Fiona's grandparents now live on a larger island, where they and their McConville relatives had been forced to move when Fiona's father left them. Following her doctor's advice to recover her health, Fiona goes back to Ron Mor Isle and visits her grandparents. She has another plan for herself during her stay with them: to look for the lost brother Jamie, whom a strong current of the sea had taken away from his father's hand when the father tried to take the boy with his family to the city. Fiona later finds that Jamie has long been protected by seals.

In Fry's story seals are protectors of Fiona, her cousin Rolie and her grandparents as well as her brother Jamie: the 'Chieftain' seal is their chief guardian. The lives of the McConvilles, (young and old) – on the island and while they are sailing on the sea – are always watched over by the Chieftain seal. The Chieftain seal in this story is – just as the horse in *St. Mawr* is – a visitor from 'another world', an animal or a fairy world, whose tie had been cut from Fiona for four years: Fiona, now 10 years old, had left the island at the age of six. When she comes back the Chieftain seal and his companions welcome her into their animal world. While she looks for Jamie her cousin and grandparents also share the community of the girl and the seals. When they all decide to go back to their original home island from the present location the seals are also pleased with their happy reunion there (with all these descendants of the seal-woman).

Fry suggests, in making a brief reference to 'the sound of a (church) bell' (46), that Fiona's social background is the Christian world, yet her contact with the seals and seagulls on the islands brings Fiona and her relatives that happy coexistence with the sea creatures which the Christian world fails to give them. Thus in *Child of the Western Isles,* too, the animistic world is revived in the modern world. Since the animistic world view is what Christianity fails to evaluate Fry turns to the old Celtic wisdom of vivid life, just as Lawrence turns to European animism (whether Greco-Roman, Celtic, or Egyptian) in *St. Mawr* and *The Escaped Cock.* This is so that modern people can recover or remember, at least, the vivid sense of being alive in nature by having immediate contact with it – just as ancient people did.

v

The modern age – which is characterized by homo-centricism or material prosperity – disregards or suppresses the world of gods or the animistic world and tries instead to establish the dominating power of humans over nature (as well as seeking ever-increasing material prosperity by destroying natural environments inhabited by the gods). Consequently, the animistic world has been lost. However, Lou's or Isis's woman or Fiona's recovery of animism is – in other words – Lawrence's or Fry's rejection or denial of the modern homo-centric values. Lawrence's and Fry's statements can be said to be modern acts of searching for a different value from the moderns. Lou, Isis's woman and Fiona may be called modern female seekers or aspirants to a vital life by returning to the old animistic worldview. They are full of a pagan sense of vitality and are fully acknowledged as such in the stories. It is worth noticing that women and girls, not men and boys, are given more important roles in *St. Mawr, The Escaped Cock* and *Child of the Western Isles*. Since they are or get to be deeply rooted in Mother Earth or nature, their vivid sense of life works fully in the animistic world.

Lawrence's other attempt to recover animism in the modern world is found in *The Plumed Serpent.* Yet it is an attempt to recover the animism of the Mexican Indians in Mexico, not European animism, and it is in contrast with the destructive force of western Christianity (which eradicated the Indians' belief in gods such as Quetzalcoatl or Huitzilopochtli). This novel

86

would be better discussed in the wider perspective of a counter-attack of the suppressed animistic worldview of the Indians against the destructive and dominating power of western Christianity in Mexico. I have therefore excluded the Mexican novel from the present discussion, focusing instead on the modern revival of European animism which is vividly described both by Lawrence in *St. Mawr* and *The Escaped Cock* and by Fry in *Child of the Western Isles*.

CHAPTER 8

LAWRENCE'S PAN WORSHIP AND GREEN MAN IMAGE

i

D. H. Lawrence was not only a writer but also a painter. As a writer he wrote many works in which he made many references to his Pan worship or nature worship. As a painter he began to paint many nude paintings energetically, especially after 1926. In 1929 his nude paintings were exhibited in the Dorothy Warren Gallery in London: soon after the exhibition, many of them were confiscated by the police because of their nudity. Among the exhibited paintings there was an interesting painting called 'Red Willow Trees', which was painted in 1927[1] and depicts, it seems to me, a Green Man image: an archetypal image of man and tree in oneness, as well as a paradisiacal state. The purpose of this chapter is to clarify the unique features of the 1927 painting by relating its Green Man image with Lawrence's Pan worship or nature worship in his literary works, because Lawrence's Green Man image in that painting has not received any critical attention from critics (Harry T. Moore, Jack Lindsay, Herbert Read, Robert W. Millett etc.). As for the Green Man image John B. Humma, in his essay on *Kangaroo,* briefly referred to the gamekeeper Oliver Mellors in *Lady Chatterley's Lover* (1928) 'as a more fully developed Green Man' than Richard L. Somers just wearing green in *Kangaroo* (1923) (Humma 516). I argue that the Green Man, another form of Pan, would be found in the painting 'Red Willow Trees', too. The painting also seems to be a pictorial representation of that paradisiacal state which Connie and Mellors attain in the forest in *Lady Chatterley's Lover*.

ii

First, let us make a brief survey of Lawrence's Pan worship or nature worship in his literary works (from his earliest work to the last). In one of the earliest poems, 'The Wild Common', (which was first published in

Amores in 1916) vivid life is depicted with nature imagery, such as flame-like gorse bushes and sweeping peewits:

> The quick sparks on the gorse bushes are leaping,
> Little jets of sunlight texture imitating flame;
> Above them, exultant, the peewits are sweeping:
> They are lords of the desolate wastes of sadness their scream-
>   ings proclaim.
> (*Amores* 4; *CP* 894) (*Poems* 5, where the fourth line reads, as in *CP* 33:
> 'They have triumphed again o'er the ages, their screamings proclaim.'
> In *Poems* 'peewits' is spelt as 'pee-wits')

It should be noted that a Lawrentian characteristic, such as the flame image of gorse bushes or the peewits as lords of the life of the wild common, is already evident as early as in this poem.

The second stanza of the poem is characterized by life-flow between rabbits and a hill:

> Rabbits, handfuls of brown earth, lie
> Low-rounded on the mournful turf they have bitten down to
> 　the quick.
> Are they asleep? – Are they alive? – Now see, when I
> Move my arms, the hill bursts and heaves under their spurting
> 　kick!
> (*Amores* 4; *CP* 894) (*Poems* 5, where 'Move' is replaced with
> 　'Lift')

The moment the poet lifts his arms he feels vital life flowing between the rabbits and the hill: the flux of life is again a very Lawrentian feature.

In 1928 when Lawrence revised this poem to include it in his edition of *The Collected Poems* he added the following new stanza:

> But how splendid it is to be substance, here!
> My shadow is neither here nor there; but I, I am royally here!
> I am here! I am here! screams the peewit; the may-blobs burst
> 　out in a laugh as they hear!

> Here! flick the rabbits. Here! pants the gorse. Here! say the
> insects far and near. (*CP* 34) (*Poems* 6, where 'peewit is
> spelt as 'pee-wit' (as in the first stanza))

In this added stanza not only the poet but other living things have vivid 'substance' as a vital part of nature. Though the poet sees each living thing with his eyes he feels its life intuitively, and vividly depicts it in words. Lawrence's intuitive awareness of each 'substance' in this stanza exactly corresponds with his insightful appreciation of Cézanne's paintings in his 1929 essay 'Introduction to These Paintings', in which he indicates: 'He (Cézanne) wanted to touch the world of substance once more with the intuitive touch, to be aware of it with intuitive awareness, and to express it in intuitive terms' (*LEA* 211). Similarly, in the above 1928 stanza Lawrence wants to express 'the world of substance' 'with intuitive awareness'. What matters most to the poet Lawrence (just as to the painter Cézanne) is not 'our present mode of mental-visual consciousness' but 'a mode of consciousness that was predominantly intuitive, the awareness of touch' (*LEA* 211), or to put it more precisely again in Lawrence's words, not 'mental consciousness' but 'blood consciousness' (*L* ii 470).

Every creature's joy of being alive is successfully represented in that 1928 stanza. If that joyous sense of the stanza is pictorialised on a canvas we will have Lawrence's painting of the same year called 'Dance Sketch', (Figure 1) (Sagar, *D. H. Lawrence's Paintings* 62) in which a man, a woman and a goat joyfully dance as living substances of nature in a forest. If the poet's sense of natural life in the 1916 version of 'The Wild Common' is not called Pan-worship it is at least called nature reverence, which is keenly felt by the poet. However, the 1928 stanza of 'The Wild Common' could be thematically considered together with 'Dance Sketch' – which certainly suggests Lawrence's Pan worship – because a dancing goat in the painting suggests Pan himself, whose legs are those of a goat (Millett 100). As this painting shows, in 1928 Lawrence still had a vivid image of Pan, though Patricia Merivale says that 'by 1928 Pan's vitality was exhausted and Lawrence willingly relinquished the image' (Merivale 217).

In Lawrence's earliest novel *The White Peacock* (1911) his nature worship is vividly represented. The narrator and hero Cyril (who left his native town of Nethermere and now lives and 'suffer(s) acutely the sickness of exile'(*WP* 260) in Norwood, a London suburb), is haunted by a spirit of Nethermere and finds himself crying for the valley of the native place.

> For weeks I wandered the streets of the suburb, haunted by the spirit of some part of Nethermere (…) A strange voice within me rose and called for the hill-path; again I could feel the wood waiting for me, calling and calling, and I crying for the wood, yet the space of many miles was between us. (*WP* 260)

Cyril's feeling is not only a nostalgic feeling towards his native town but a manifest example of his nature worship because he feels, even in the metropolis, the spirit of his native town. In *The White Peacock*, however, Lawrence was not as confident of the mythic role of the gamekeeper Annable as a Pan-like figure or a Green Man, because he is soon killed in an accident and disappears from the text.

However, when Lawrence read James G. Frazer's *The Golden Bough* and *Totemism and Exogamy* in 1915 he was convinced of the primitive consciousness or 'blood consciousness' (*L* ii 470), and as John B. Vickery indicates in *The Literary Impact of* The Golden Bough (294), Lawrence began to introduce various mythic themes in his works in much confidence. In *St. Mawr* (1925), for example, Lawrence's Pan-motif and nature worship are more confidently and vividly presented than in *The White Peacock*: one day in her dull life in London with her lifeless husband Rico Carrington, Lou sees a horse called St. Mawr and is deeply impressed with its vital life. For her St. Mawr is not only 'some splendid demon' (*StM* 31) but also 'Pan', as she later acknowledges (*StM* 66). The encounter with St. Mawr is a clear example of Lou's Pan worship, which is in stark contrast to her husband's lifelessness. Then she buys the horse to have him at her side. St. Mawr, instead of Rico, gives her a vivid sense of life.

When Lou goes back to America with St. Mawr she finds a ranch in Arizona, where she feels a wild spirit of place bigger than men and religion:

> It's something more real to me than men are, and it soothes
> me, and it holds me up. It's something wild, that will hurt
> me sometimes and will wear me down sometimes. I know it.
> But it's something big, bigger than men, bigger than people,
> bigger than religion. (*StM* 155)

And she is determined to live on this ranch to live with the spirit that 'has
waited (for her) so long' there: she says that it is her 'mission' to keep
herself for 'the spirit that is wild'. (*StM* 155)

Thus, in the novella, Lou is rescued by St. Mawr as Pan in England
and finds it her mission to live with the spirit of place in America (and
refusing life with Rico, her lifeless husband).

Rico and Lou Carrington in *St. Mawr* prefigure Clifford and Connie
Chatterley in *Lady Chatterley's Lover*. The character who rescues Connie
in Lawrence's last novel is not a horse as Pan but the vital life of nature in
a forest and a gamekeeper as Pan-believer. In the novel Connie, whose life
had been exhausted by her husband's egocentrism, feels a life-awakening
power in a forest and finds a tree's vital life flowing into her body:

> Connie sat down with her back in a young pine-tree, that swayed
> against her with curious life, elastic and powerful rising up. The
> erect alive thing, with its top in the sun! And she watched the daffo-
> dils go sunny in a burst of sun, that was warm on her hands and lap.
> Even she caught the faint tarry scent of the flowers. (*LCL* 86)

Connie is here in oneness with the pine tree, the sun and the daffodils.
Connie's tree sense could be regarded as a development of Lawrence's
earlier tree life experience which is evident in his early poem called 'Corot',
in which the life of 'magnificent trees' is strongly felt by the poet:

> Ah listen, for Silence is not lonely:
> Imitate the magnificent trees
> That speak no word of their rapture, but only
> Breathe largely the luminous breeze.
> (*Love Poems* 34; cf. *Poems* 37, where 'Silence' is spelt with a
>   small letter s)

The poet's sense of the life of 'the magnificent trees' is further deepened by Connie, who feels the pine tree as '(the) erect alive thing' and its 'elastic and powerful' life. Besides, she is in interrelatedness with the sun and the daffodils, reclining against the tree. Her life is quickened by the tree, sun and daffodils. Such powerful natural life is referred to as 'Pan' later in the novel by the gamekeeper Mellors:

> They (the mass of people) should be alive and frisky, and acknowledge the great god Pan. He's the only god for the masses, forever. The few can go in for higher cults if they like. But let the masses be forever pagan. (*LCL* 300)

Since the gamekeeper is the only man of the forest in the novel he is depicted not only as a typical example of the Green Man, as Humma indicates, but as an embodiment of Pan-power of the forest: as such Mellors acts first as Connie's saviour and later as her partner.

iii

In his essays Lawrence made a clear statement of his own Pan worship. As early as 1913, when Lawrence wrote a book review of *Georgian Poetry 1911–1912* (Poplawski 4), he already expressed his Pan worship, saying: 'I worship Pan' as well as 'Christ', 'Jehovah', and 'Aphrodite' because 'I need them all, all gods'. (*IR* 204)

His belief of such deities was strengthened, as we have indicated, by reading Frazer's anthropological works in 1915. When Lawrence feels the power of tree life, he often tells us about his own tree worship or Pan worship. In *Fantasia of the Unconscious* (1922), for example, he feels the tremendous power of trees in the Black Forest in Germany and he says his soul is enlarged and in oneness with their life:

> A huge, plunging, tremendous soul (a tree has). I would like to be a tree for a while. The great lust of roots. Root-lust. And no mind at all. He towers, and I sit and feel safe. I like to feel him towering round me. I used to be afraid. I used to fear their lust, their rushing black lust. But now I like it, I worship it. I always felt them huge primeval enemies. But now they are my

> only shelter and strength. I lose myself among the trees. I am
> so glad to be with them to their silent, intent passion, and their
> great lust. They feed my soul. (*FU* 86–7)

The same belief is repeated in other essays: in 'Aristocracy' and in 'Pan
in America', too. In 'Aristocracy ', which was written in 1925 (Poplawski
30), he feels a great oak tree alive with life and he says 'you should worship
him': that is, worship Pan in the oak tree.

> And the oak-tree, the slow great oak-tree, isn't he alive? Doesn't
> he live where you *don't* live, with a vast silence you shall never,
> never penetrate, though you chop him into kindling shred from
> shred. He is alive with life such as you have not got and will
> never have. And in so far as he is a vast, powerful, silent life,
> you should worship him. (*RDP* 372) (Lawrence's italics)

One year earlier than 'Aristocracy' (Poplawski 37), 'Pan in America' was
written in Taos, New Mexico, while he stayed there with Frieda in a cabin.
Above and in front of the cabin, he says, a big pine tree rose up 'like a
guardian spirit' (*MM* 157). As Lawrence says in the essay, at the beginning
of the Christian era it was said that Pan was dead; and then the old Pan 'was
turned into the devil of the Christians' (*MM* 157). However, Lawrence says
that Pan is not dead for him: Pan, who had been degraded from pagan
fertility god to Christian devil for centuries, is still vividly living in the pine
tree in old America and (just as Lou Carrington intuits Pan in the horse St.
Mawr in the novella) Lawrence himself feels the Pan-power in the tree in
the American essay:

> It vibrates its presence into my soul, and I am with Pan. I think
> no man could live near a pine tree and remain quite suave
> and supple and compliant. Something fierce and bristling is
> communicated. The piney sweetness is rousing and defiant,
> like turpentine, the noise of the needles is keen with aeons of
> sharpness. (*MM* 158)

'Pan in America' is the most manifest statement of Lawrence's Pan worship.

iv

After leaving New Mexico in 1925 Lawrence went to Italy, the climate of which was chosen for his weakening health, and he stayed in the Villa Mirenda near Florence. There he started his painting energetically in 1926 when he received 'four rather large used canvases' from Maria Huxley,[2] and painted, in particular, various nude paintings. And in June 1929 his 25 paintings were exhibited in the Dorothy Warren gallery, London. During the exhibition 13 paintings out of the 25 were confiscated by police because of their nudity and display of pubic hair: Robert W. Millett comments on the confiscation in his pioneering work on Lawrence's paintings, *The Vultures and the Phoenix*:

> The sole criterion for the choice of paintings to be confiscated seems to have been whether pubic hair was in evidence in the painting. No question of artistic merit or artistic intention seems to have been operative at any time. (Millett 16)

One of the exhibited 25 paintings was 'Red Willow Trees' (Figure 2) (Sagar, *D. H. Lawrence's Paintings* 34) which was not taken away from the gallery by the police, probably because it did not depict pubic hair.

'Red Willow Trees' looks like a very strange painting because a man's head on the left-hand side seems to possess the boughs of a tree, while he sits on its lower bough. On this painting Harry T. Moore briefly says that it is 'formally satisfying' (Moore 17), while Millett points out the unique feature of its composition:

> (...) the landscape element is the most dominant feature. The figures of the three male nudes bathing are almost unobtrusive. They are placed in the foreground and off centre. Only one figure is standing and, in a sense, it is only this figure that commands attention from the viewer. The other figures are completely overshadowed by the expanse of the flowing landscape. (Millett 46)

And Millett detects '(the) influence of Cézanne' (46) in this painting because Cézanne had painted a male bather series. Millett concludes that 'in terms of composition and technique, it is fairly successful' (46).

But neither of the critics pays attention to the strange head of the standing man. However, Keith Sagar, in the 'Introduction' to his edition of *D. H. Lawrence's Paintings*, makes an interesting and suggestive comment about the man's head: 'the figure on the left is positioned in such a way that the boughs of the willow seem to be branching out from his head. Perhaps Lawrence is remembering his own image from the poem 'A Doe at Evening': "being a male, is not my head hard-balanced, antlered?"[3] As Sagar aptly observes, the boughs seem to stick out from the man's head. Here I would like to go further with his interpretation: I suggest that the man's head from which the boughs seem to stick out is Lawrence's pictorial version of the Green Man image.

Lawrence's Green Man image in the painting seems to be a modern echo of the traditional and archetypal image in European aesthetics: originally, various figures of the image were often carved or placed on or in church buildings or architecture, and the Green Man image symbolizes a man who lives in harmony with a tree or with nature. That image is often depicted as a man's face (which is covered with tree leaves).

Let us look at four examples (which are Clive Hicks' photographs in Andersen's book). Two examples (Figures 3 and 4) (Anderson's illustration nos. 20 and 85) show that a woman's or man's head is almost covered with tree leaves. Each head is set deeply within the leaves and she or he has close contact with them: that is, natural life. The other two examples (Figures 5 and 6) (Anderson's illustration nos. 8 and 13) show that a branch or branches stick out from the head of a man or woman. All these figures are classified as a Green Man (or Woman). Although the term Green Man was first introduced to explain its images in church art by Lady Raglan in 1939 the Green Man is, '(in) his origins', 'much older than our Christian era'. This is indicated by William Anderson in his book, *Green Man: the Archetype of our Oneness with the Earth* (14), and the Green Man image has been used 'for the past 2,000 years' (Anderson 14). Although it had been used since ancient times many images of the Green Man were often fashioned in or on church buildings, especially in the medieval period: the Green Man often appears in English folklore, too, according to Simpson and Roud's *Dictionary of English Folklore* (154). The term now has often been referred to in the discussion of the relationship between man and natural environments and has a very significant ecological implication.

When we think about the symbolic meaning of the Green Man it certainly symbolizes the unity of man and nature. Or, to use a mythological term, it represents the living relationship between man and Pan or man and Mother Earth. As we have observed above, Pan as fertility god was once expelled out of the imagination of the Europeans after it was said that Pan was dead. However, the exterminated Pan was revived in another form of Green Man (especially in the medieval period and later periods) as Anderson fully exemplifies in his book. It is paradoxical that many Green Man images were often carved on or in church buildings. The imagination of the Europeans definitely needed another Pan in the form of the Green Man after the announcement of Pan's death, and many anonymous artists were tempted to carve Green Man figures on or in church buildings. Therefore, Christianity, (which once denied the pagan fertility god Pan) newly introduced its own version of Pan in the form of the Green Man with a man's face covered with tree leaves.

The archetypal Green Man image, it seems to me, is revived not only in the gamekeeper Mellors, as Humma points out, but in the naked man with boughs on his head in Lawrence's 'Red Willow Trees'. The man in the painting, therefore, can be said to be a Lawrentian version of the Green Man or a disguised Pan: or, when viewed with James Frazer's *The Golden Bough*, 'Red Willow Trees' is also reminiscent of Attis (an ancient 'tree spirit' or 'spirit of vegetation' (Frazer 352)) or 'Green George' (who was covered with willow leaves, who was believed to communicate his festival participants' 'vital energy') (Frazer 127). In every case, the painting suggests Lawrence's nature worship or Pan worship, and its artistic feature is in complete accordance with the same nature worship or Pan worship in his various literary works which we have seen above).

What is more, the man with the boughs sticking from his head and the two bathing men in the painting are placed in harmony with, in Millett's words, 'the flowing landscape' (46) or the landscape with the biblical 'pure river of water of life' (*Rev.* 22:1) flowing across it. In other words it symbolically represents a paradisiacal state of men, without any consciousness of nakedness. If so, it is in parallel with another paradisiacal state – which is attained by Connie and Mellors, who dance naked in the rain in a forest in *Lady Chatterley's Lover* (221), and which was written around the same period as when 'Red Willow Trees' was painted. While 'Red Willow Trees' does not depict a woman Lawrence's other painting 'Dance Sketch' depicts (as we have seen) a dancing woman with a goat which suggests Pan and, since the latter painting shows (as Sagar indicates) 'the paradise of at-oneness',[4] it naturally reminds us of the dancing scene of Connie and Mellors with his dog Flossie running around them in *Lady Chatterley's Lover* (Kouno 173). 'Red Willow Trees' (as well as 'Dance Sketch') depicts a paradisiacal state which is quite similar to that in *Lady Chatterley's Lover*.

Thus, in conclusion, the 1927 painting 'Red Willow Trees' is at once both a representation of a Lawrentian version of the Green Man or Pan worship and a pictorial depiction of the paradisiacal state which Lawrence tries to create in his 1928 novel *Lady Chatterley's Lover*.

Notes
1. Keith Sagar, 'Introduction', *D. H. Lawrence's Paintings*, ed. Keith Sagar, p. 34.
2. Sagar, 'Introduction', p. 29. See also D. H. Lawrence, 'Making Pictures', *Late Essays and Articles*, p. 227.
3. Sagar, 'Introduction', p. 36.
4. Sagar, 'Introduction', p. 63.

Figure 1: *'Dance Sketch'*

Figure 2: *'Red Willow Trees'*

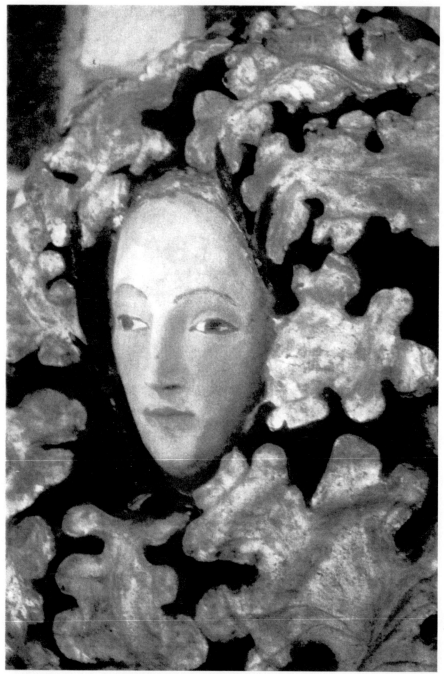
Figure 3: *'Anderson's illustration no.20'*

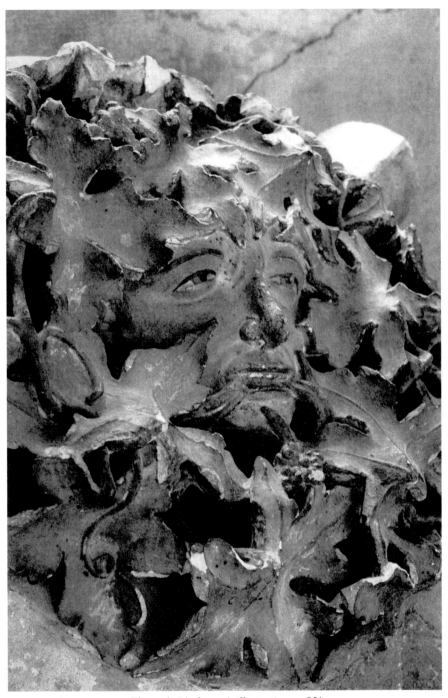

Figure 4: *'Anderson's illustration no.85'*

Figure 5: *'Anderson's illustration no.8'*

Figure 6: *'Anderson's illustration no.13'*

CHAPTER 9

THE UNIVERSALITY OF LAWRENCE'S ANIMISTIC VISION

i

D. H. Lawrence's animistic perception can be seen in the encounters with such a living thing as a doe, a snake, a fox, a tree etc. It is not the peculiar phenomenon of an eccentric or perverse Englishman, but a universal one. The purpose of this chapter is to demonstrate the universality of Lawrence's animistic vision by comparing it with Japanese and ancient European animistic visions.

First we will take up Lawrence's five works: one story, two poems and two essays. These are: *The Fox*, 'A Doe at Evening', 'Snake', *Fantasia of the Unconscious* and 'Pan in America', all of which show his animistic perception in encounters with living things. In correspondence with the fox, the doe, the snake and the tree we will then consider four Japanese examples of animistic perception. These are: the legend called 'The Fox-wife in the Forest of Shinoda', the modern Japanese writer Keiji Sunouchi's Japanese version of the Lawrentian vision of deer, an ancient Japanese snake myth and the modern Japanese poet Kazue Morisaki's Lawrentian vision of the tree. These Japanese examples show that Lawrence's animistic perception is not only a local one but a universal one. The African San Bushman's animism will also be referred to in the discussion, to indicate the connection between Bushman's animism and Lawrence's animism. To demonstrate further the universality and the basic root of Lawrence's animistic vision we will finally take up an English folktale called 'The Woman of the Sea', an English ballad called 'The Great Silkie of Sule Skerry' and the Green Man image tradition. These will all reveal that Lawrence's animistic perception goes far back, to the tradition of ancient European animism (which has been suppressed or obscured by the traditions of dominant Christianity and Cartesian rationalism). European animistic tradition, however, reasserts itself through Lawrence's writings as life-awakening power (which has been weakened by rigid Christianity and rationalism) as is demonstrated in *The Escaped Cock* (157–8) and *Apocalypse* (78). Some critics have paid attention to *The Fox*, 'A Doe at Evening', and 'Snake' from the viewpoint of sexuality (H. Mori 198–201; Hagen 40). However, such an interpretation will overlook the animistic aspect of these works (which I would like to clarify here).

ii

In *The Fox*, the fox infiltrates the farm of March and Banford, seeking for a prey with its sharp eyes. He is called 'a demon' (9), because he 'carried off the hens under the very nose of March and Banford' (9). However, the fox is not always a destructive demon in the story, because it is given a double meaning: evil demon and mysterious daemon. To March, the fox later appears to be an animal of 'spell-power' (12), and he is so mysterious an animal that March is 'spell-bound' (10). Furthermore, she is intuitively united with him: 'they (the fox's eyes) met her eyes. And he knew her. She was spell-bound – she knew he knew her' (10). As long as March is fascinated by the fox's mysterious eyesight or spell he is not an evil demon. Instead, the fox is felt by March as a sort of daemon or deity, a definition originally implied by the word demon in *The Oxford English Dictionary*[1]. This is March's animistic perception, awakened by the fox as daemon. Thus the fox has a powerful hold on March, which means that the fox gradually replaces the position of Banford in March's life, as she has previously been put under Banford's control and is kept in a lesbian relationship with her.

The appearance of the fox is a prelude to the appearance of the more important character: Henry. Henry is 'identified with the fox' (18) and the spell of the fox is, therefore, inherited by Henry in the story. That is, the fox's life power dwells in Henry – who is finally united with March and who casts out Banford from March's life circuit – just as the fox did, previously. The daemonic power of the fox is shared both by Henry and March and, therefore, they have a vivid sense of fox animism. This first awakens March's life-awareness and rescues her from her imprisoned lesbian relationship with Banford and then succeeds in establishing the vital union with Henry, though she is not necessarily satisfied with the new relationship with him at the end of the story.

The sense of animism is presented more straightforwardly in Lawrence's poems, 'A Doe at Evening' and 'Snake'. In 'A Doe at Evening' Lawrence is intuitively united with a doe when he sees it face to face in a marsh:

> I looked at her
> and felt her watching;
> I became a strange being.
> Still, I had my right to be there with her.
>
> Her nimble shadow
> along a sky-line,
> put back her fine, level-balanced head.
> And I knew her. (*Poems* 180–81)

Here the doe casts a strong spell on him, because Lawrence says that he 'became a strange being'. The doe facing the poet is not just an ordinary animal but is felt as a mysterious being, and this is another example of Lawrence's animistic perception.

In this poem Lawrence does not use the word god or deity to describe the mysterious doe. Its godliness is implied by the strange and sudden encounter itself. In 'Snake', however, a snake is clearly felt as a god. Lawrence first welcomes it when it comes to a water trough as a guest. And then the snake looks 'like a god' (*Poems* 304) when it looks around contentedly after drinking water. Though the poet feels honoured to have the guest it suddenly occurs to him that the venomous snake must be killed, and he throws a stick at it. In this instant the poet is torn between two opposite feelings: an animistic one and an anti-animistic or homo-centric one. But finally the poet finds himself to be wrong:

> And immediately I regretted it.
> I thought how paltry, how vulgar, what a mean act!
> I despised myself and the voices of my accursèd human education.
> (*Poems* 305)

And thus, the snake is no longer felt as an enemy. It looks like a king to be crowned again:

(…) he seemed to me again like a king,
Like a king in exile, uncrowned in the underworld,
Now due to be crowned again. (*Poems* 305)

And, finally, the poet considers the snake to be 'one of the lords / Of life' (*Poems* 305): in other words, a god of life. Thus, the poet, despising the voices of the 'accursed human education', namely homo-centric or anti-animistic voices, rescues and reevaluates his own animistic sense.

According to the Christian doctrine the snake is always a symbol of evil, and Lawrence nearly accepts this when he throws a stick at the snake to kill it. However, when he later sloughs off his prejudice against the snake and accepts his animistic vision as it is, he makes up for what Christian doctrine lacks. He challenges, to use Keith Sagar's words, 'two thousand years of Christianity' (*Life into Art* 236) which have robbed the snake of its place, and he tries to summon it back to take (its) place as 'one of the lords of life'(237).

When Lawrence wrote the poem 'Snake' (as well as other poems in *Birds, Beasts and Flowers*) he had absorbed, Christopher Heywood indicates (151–61), many ideas in embryo from the African San Bushman's animism in *Specimens of Bushman Folklore* (which he borrowed from the South African artist Jan Juta and read in 1920). When he was influenced by African animism, as Heywood argues, his animistic perception of a snake (for example) was sharply stimulated and vitalised by it. This produced the poem 'Snake' which is, as Vivian de Sola Pinto points out, 'a rare and memorable achievement' (13) and 'one of the very few English poems in free verse' (14). San Bushman's and Lawrence's snake animism are very close to each other (as Heywood discusses) and, more importantly, they possess much universality. Besides, Lawrence – as a modern European – uniquely dramatises the conflict between the Christian way of thinking and the animistic way of thinking, which he finally restores in the modern age in the poem. Thus the vital sense of animism has, in Lawrence's work, its own unique place – which should not be obscured or distorted by any centuries-old Christian prejudice.

Lawrence's animistic perception works not only in encounters with animals but also with plants. In *Fantasia of the Unconscious* (85–6), he feels the life power of the trees in the Black Forest of Germany. While he sits beneath a tree in the forest he feels the life-blood of the tree running into his fingers, and he realizes the deep meaning of the tree worship of the ancient Aryan races. He finds himself to be a tree worshipper. In his essay 'Pan in America' (*MM* 157–8) too, he feels the all-inclusiveness of Pan-power in the pine trees under which his cabin stands. He thinks the Pan-power has not died out yet. This is a modern revival of Aryan or ancient Greek animism.

iii

In the Japanese legend known as 'The Fox-wife in the Forest of Shinoda' (Takeda 4–9), the young man called Yasuna becomes desperate and forlorn after his lover Sakakinomae commits suicide because she, though innocent, was severely accused of an unjustified crime against her master. While Yasuna is wandering aimlessly in the forest of Shinoda a woman resembling Sakakinomae appears to him and tells him that she is Sakakinomae's sister, and that she is called Kuzunoha. His love is revived and he is attracted strongly to Kuzunoha, who begins to love him too. However, an evil man called Akuuemon gets her away from Yasuna by force, badly harming him. When the wounded Yasuna has lost his aim in life a female fox – hastily taking the form of the woman Kuzunoha – appears to him to take care of his wounds, because once the fox was rescued by Yasuna when she was caught by Akuuemon in the forest of Shinoda. In return for Yasuna's kindness the fox-woman has taken the form of Kuzunoha, to console him. Even after Yasuna's wounds are cured the fox-woman never leaves him, and soon they get married and have a child. Yasuna has no idea of the identity of his wife, thinking that she is indeed Kuzunoha herself.

When the boy reaches five years old the real Kuzunoha, who has herself fallen passionately in love with Yasuna, visits him with her parents to ask him for permission to get married to her. Yasuna is surprised to be asked for the marriage with her because he thinks that he had been married to Kuzunoha for five years. He wonders who the two identical Kuzunohas are. When Yasuna asks his wife who she really is she explains that she is not a human but the fox who had been saved by him and, transforming herself into Kuzunoha, appeared in order to console him. When the real woman Kuzunoha appears in front of Yasuna the fox-wife immediately realizes that she must leave him and their five-year-old son and go back to the forest of Shinoda as a fox.

In this story fox and man live together happily for five years, and the fox is regarded not only as a benefactor to a human but as a kind creature with an anima: the fox and man are treated as equal beings. Even after the fox leaves her son she writes a *Waka* poem for him, saying that if he longs to see her he can come to the forest of Shinoda whenever he likes (though she is now forced to leave him with great sorrow). The fox-mother does not lose her motherly love for her son at the moment of saddest separation. It is evident that the background of this story is an animistic world view.

In Lawrence's tale *The Fox*, the fox or fox power dwells in March and Henry, and March achieves an intuitive unity with the fox when she knows him. In 'The Fox-wife in the Forest of Shinoda' the fox-wife truly gets married to a man and they live together. Both stories are characterized by an animistic sense.

In 'A Doe at Evening', Lawrence meets a doe in the evening in the marsh and is spellbound and he 'knew her' (*Poems* 181). This is again an intuitive union with her and an animistic revelation. The Japanese modern writer Keiji Sunouchi had a very similar experience when he went up a mountain one day and had a sudden encounter with a deer. He recalls his strange experience: 'when I met a deer face to face in the mountain, I suddenly felt him a god. He looked a divine being, standing so still. I could not move at all' (*The Wind Blows* 113: my translation). Comparing Sunouchi's experience with Lawrence's, the former sounds very Lawrentian. Moreover, the Japanese writer was more awestruck than Lawrence was in 'A Doe at Evening' where he does not explicitly say the doe is a god, while Sunouchi felt the deer was a god. Lawrence's other poem 'Snake' shows that he also had an awestruck experience when he saw a snake, as we have seen above. In this poem the snake is felt as a god of life.

In a Japanese snake myth a snake gets married to a woman. According to the myth, a young man visits a woman every night and sleeps with her, without showing his face. Wondering who he is, one day her parents trace a thread (which he left behind). The thread leads up to a mountain called Mount Miwa where the parents find out that the young man is, in fact, a snake who lives in the mountain and who is worshipped as a god. The snake transformed himself into a young man and visited the woman every night (*Kojiki* 203–04). As far as the snake deity is concerned the snake in this myth is a god to be worshipped, just as in Lawrence's poem, 'Snake'.

Needless to say, Japanese animism is not confined to animal encounters. The modern Japanese poet Kazue Morisaki intuits the divine power of a tree. She feels 'a spirit of place' (*The Prayer of the Earth* 18: my translation) when she sees a 200-year-old birch tree in a forest. Her perception is so much sharpened by the old powerful tree that she feels its spirit or 'Eros'. In the poem entitled 'A Spirit of Place', she says:

> A birch tree has a female flower and a male flower,
> birch tree.
>
> … … … .
> You naked birch tree,
> Two-hundred-year-old tree,
> I touch my cheek on your skin,
> I entrust myself on you,
> And close my eyes.
> My love song runs through your twigs.
> Are you a female or male?
> Water is drumming through within your soft skin,
> The sound of water is full of Eros.
> (*The Prayer of the Earth* 18–19: my translation)

In this poem Morisaki considers Eros to be a primitive life power and she places herself in the life-flow between the birch tree and herself, enjoying life-communication between them. The tree life comes into her and her life into the tree, and thus she and the tree are in oneness. Their union is suggested by a sexual image. Her living union with the tree is just like the interpenetration between Lawrence's life and tree life in 'Pan in America' (25) or like Lawrence's union with a doe in the evening. Their unions are both very animistic.

iv

Unlike the snake in the book of Genesis of the Bible the snake in the ancient Greek myth of Aesculapius – the god of the medical art – was 'sacred to him' because it was 'a symbol of renovation' and was believed 'to have the power of discovering herbs' (Peck, *Harper's Dictionary* 37). In the same myth the snake coils itself around the staff of the physician Aesculapius as his helpful assistant (Peck 37), but never gets married to a woman. An English ballad and folktale, however, show an animal and a human as equal marriage partners. In the ballad 'The Great Silkie of Sule Skerry' a seal-man proposes marriage to a woman but predicts to her that he and their future child between them will be shot by her second husband:

> And thu sall marry a proud gunner,
> An a proud gunner I'm sure he'll be,
> An the very first schot that ere he schoots,
> He'll schoot baith my young son and me. (Sargent and
> Kittredge 240)[2]

Although this ballad hints at the marriage between the seal-man and the woman it does not state that the seal-man gets married to the woman, because the ballad ends with that prediction. On the other hand, in the folk tale known as 'The Woman of the Sea' (Crossley-Holland 39–42)[3], a seal-woman really gets married to a man. It is said that seals can transform themselves into humans and remain in human shape as long as they take off their sealskins. In the folk tale 'The Woman of the Sea' seal-women, having cast off their sealskins on the beach, are bathing in the sea. A young man who chances to see them bathing steals the sealskin of one seal-woman. The seal-woman implores him to give her skin back to her because otherwise she cannot go back to the sea, but the young man does not believe her and asks her to become his wife. Since the seal-woman cannot take the form of a seal and go back to the sea without the sealskin, she finally consents to the young man's proposal and gets married to him. They have three children and lead a happy life. But one day the seal-wife finds the sealskin by chance (which had been hidden in some hay by her husband), and immediately she puts it on: she leaves him and the three children and goes back to the sea. In the folk tale the seal-wife and the young man live together happily for a few years and the seal-wife is a benefactor to a human, just like the fox-wife in the Japanese legend. The world of the seal-woman folk tale is far removed from Christian ideology, which places human beings in a superior position to animals and therefore does not give the same status to animals as it does to man (as this folk tale does). Evidently the world of this folk tale is not of Christianity but of animism, which was of pre-Christian origin and not extinguished by the power of Christianity.

The seal-woman folk tale is of animal animism. Besides, there is a long tradition of tree worship in Europe, too: its archetypal image is the Green Man. William Anderson fully exemplifies it in his book entitled *Green Man*. As he demonstrates in it the Green Man image originated from 'the matriarchal religion of the Neolithic period of the first farmers centred on and around the Danube Basin' (Anderson 34) who regarded man as part of the Great Mother Earth, and this image lived on in Europe without being extinguished – even under the dominant power of Christianity: its images are engraved on churches or other buildings or in various paintings. The modern version of Lawrence's tree worship in *Fantasia of the Unconscious* and 'Pan in America' is a kind of rebirth of this ever-enduring Green Man image tradition, although he only links it with the ancient Greek myth of Pan or the Aryan tree worship of pre-Christian times.

In ancient and pre-Christian Europe animism was a dominant philosophy of life which was later suppressed by Christianity and Cartesian rationalism, and yet it survived in such a folk tale and a ballad as 'The Great Silkie of Sule Skerry' and 'The Woman of the Sea', or as Anderson shows, in a variety of Green Man images engraved on various kinds of buildings or depicted in paintings. In the 20th century it revives in Lawrence's works to provide a new and vivid life-awareness, which had been numbed by rigid Christianity and dominant rationalism. When we look at ancient European animism and Japanese animism we can conclude that Lawrence's animistic perception, even if sometimes influenced by the African San Bushman's animism, is deeply rooted in the ancient animism of Europe and that his animistic vision is not only of European origin but also of universal width and depth, as is seen in African animism or Japanese animism.

Notes:

1. The *OED* defines 'demon' as follows: 'In ancient Greek mythology: a supernatural being of a nature intermediate between that of gods and men; an inferior divinity, spirit, genius (…) Often written daemon for distinction from sense 2 (i.e., "an evil spirit").'

2 and 3 Lawrence must have read the 'great silkie' folk tale or ballad and the seal-woman folk tale, because he refers to them in *Mornings in Mexico*: 'It is the seal drifting in to the shore on the wave, or the seal-woman, singing low and secret, departing back from the shores of men, through the surf, back to the realm of the outer beasts, that rock on the waters and stare through glistening, vivid, mindless eyes' (62). See also Virginia Hyde's explanatory note to the same passage. (*MM* 259–60)

CHAPTER 10

D. H. LAWRENCE AND AKIKO YOSANO: CONTEMPORARY POETS OF HUMAN TOUCH AND COSMIC LIFE

i

Although D. H. Lawrence and the Japanese female poet Akiko Yosano (1878–1942) never met or read each other's works, they were contemporaries with similar beliefs. Lawrence and Yosano share three important features:

(1) they were leading exponents of the importance of sexuality fighting the repression of sexual desire in early 20th-century England and Japan;

(2) they defended marriage and the family; and

(3) they were tree-worshippers, sun-worshippers, and believers in cosmic life. Although they lived far apart, one in the west and the other in the east, they faced similar problems and fought against oppressive morality in order to awaken a more vivid sense of life in their countrymen.

Their common beliefs can be seen in Lawrence's *Look! We Have Come Through!* and *The Poems;* his expository prose works *Fantasia of the Unconscious* and *Apocalypse*; his essay 'Aristocracy' and his short story 'Sun'; Yosano's book of 31 syllable Tanka poems *Midaregami (Tangled Hair)*; *Selected Poems*; *Critical Essays*. Since no attention has been paid to the similarities between these two outstanding writers this chapter will clarify, from a cross-cultural point of view, the beliefs they shared as early 20th-century contemporaries. I am especially concerned with the closeness of their attitudes towards sexuality and their awareness of new western ideas about it.

ii

Some 15 years before the publication of Akiko Yosano's sensational 1901 book *Tangled Hair* two new trends in heterosexual love relations arose in Japan, which contributed to the formation of her philosophy of love between man and woman as equal and free individuals. One trend was accelerated by Yukichi Fukuzawa, the most influential philosopher of the time, who published *Danjo Kosairon* (*On the Intercourse between Man and Woman*) (1886); Tokoku Kitamura, the influential literary critic, who published his essay 'Shojono Junketsu wo Ronzu' ('On the Chastity of a Virgin') (1892); and other literary opinion leaders in influential literary journals such as *Taiyo* (*The Sun*) or *Teikokubungaku* (*Literature of the Empire*) in the 1880s and the 1890s. All these writers advocated the western idea of love, urging their readers to break away from the old fashioned Confucian morality and saying that it had suppressed spontaneous love relations between man and woman. Ohgai Mori, one of the most influential novelists, joined their campaign (though not positively) by introducing a new concept of 'sexual desire' (O. Mori 294) taken from German sexology (Saito 4). Mori, a medical doctor, had studied in Germany and was well-informed on German literature and philosophy. Among these opinion leaders Fukuzawa impressed Akiko Yosano most (as she later confessed in her 1916 essay 'Fujin no Darakusuru Saidaigenin' ('The Greatest Cause of Women's Corrruption') because he not only blamed Confucian morality for suppressing heterosexual love relations but also insisted that man and woman pursue their love relations on an equal basis, as in the west (Yosano, *Collected Works* 15: 289). He also maintained that the love relation was naturally sexual as well as spiritual (Fukuzawa, *Collected Works* 5: 589). His theory was quite new to Japanese readers, who had only known Confucian morality, and which he saw as 'social oppression' (Fukuzawa, *Collected Works* 5: 594).

Besides Fukuzawa's new theory on heterosexual love relations Akiko must have also been stimulated by new ideas concerning equality in man and woman relationships, which were energetically introduced in such well-known literary journals as *The Sun* and *Literature of the Empire* [1]. As her 1904 essay 'Hirakibumi' ('The Opened Letter') says, she had been reading these two journals (as well as other literary journals) from her early teens (Yosano, *Critical Essays* 20). In *Literature of the Empire*, for instance, Gyoro Hayakawa and anonymous literary critics encouraged Japanese writers to write a novel of new heterosexual love relations of the new age (see vol.1 No.11 (1895), 100–01; vol.2 No. 5 (1896), 102; vol.3 No. 8 (1897), 52–62). They also valued nude paintings as artistic works which should not be suppressed as obscene (see vol.5 No.6 (1899), 101). Well-known scholars such as Kunitake Kume and Yoshiharu Iwamoto (and a female critic, Namiko Sassa) contributed essays to *The Sun* urging their readers to overcome Confucian male dominance over women and to establish instead a new western-style heterosexual love relationship on an equal basis (see vol.1 No. 8 (1895), 146–54; vol.2 No. 22 (1896), 94–5; vol. 5 No. 5 (1899), 173–6; vol.5 No. 6 (1899), 159–61).

Myojo (*Morning Star*) and *Bungakukai* (*The World of Literature*) were also important journals. The former was founded in 1900 by young poet Tekkan Yosano (1873–1935), Akiko's future husband, who also questioned Confucian morality. It was not only a new Tanka poetry journal but a forum for new western artistic movements, such as art nouveau [2], and it introduced western nude paintings and drawings unfamiliar to Japanese readers. These included an anonymous painting of two women bathing in a lake (No. 5 (1900), 9); the German painter Heizoy Karl August's 'Marmorschön' (No. 8 (1900), 7); an anonymous drawing of the 'Venus de Milo' (No. 10 (1901), 36); and the Venetian painter Titian's 'Sleeping Venus' (No. 11 (1901), 5). Akiko, a reader of the new journal, was introduced to and 'strongly influenced by' (Haga 28) the new western artistic worlds. She later published her own Tanka poems in this journal, thereby allowing the editor (Tekkan) to discover her poetic genius.

Before the publication of *Morning Star* Akiko was also a reader of *The World of Literature* (Yosano, *Critical Essays* 20; see also A. Sato, *Midaregami ko* (*A Study of Tangled Hair*) 196), which was founded in 1893 by leading novelists and critics with the purpose of fighting, in a Romantic spirit, against social conservatism. *The World of Literature* also led Akiko to western nudes and other paintings. As Janine Beichman points out the July 1896 issue (No. 43) of *The World of Literature,* five years before *Morning Star,* reproduced the 16th-century Venetian painter Titian's nude painting 'Sleeping Venus', though its head only, together with a Japanese critic's article praising (against the dominant Confucian morality of the time) Titian's vivid portrayal of the nude. Beichman indicates that this painting, in the 1896 issue of *The World of Literature* (not in the 1901 issue of *Morning Star*) gave a hint to Akiko, who wrote a Tanka poem referring to Titian (Beichman 219; 306). I'll discuss this poem below. *The World of Literature* printed other western nude sketches or paintings such as 'Lady Godiva' (No. 40 (1896)), 'Love Dream' (No. 42 (1896)) and 'A Waiting Maid of Diana' (No. 58 (1898))[3], all of which Akiko must have seen before her literary debut in 1901.

The introduction of western nude paintings or sketches in *Morning Star* and *The World of Literature* shows a new Japanese awareness of sexuality, which coincided with another significant trend of late 19th-century Japan: the introduction of western sexology. Japanese doctors began to translate English and German books on sexology from the 1870s to the 1890s. The American doctor James Ashton's long-titled book was translated in 1875: *The Book of Creation: Containing Information for Young People Who Think of Getting Married, on the Philosophy of Procreation and Sexual Intercourse; Showing How to Prevent Conception and to Avoid Child-Bearing.*

The Viennese doctor Richard von Krafft-Ebing's rather sensational *Psychopathia Sexualis* was translated in 1894 and the German doctor Alfred Hegar's *Der Geschlechtstrieb: eine social medizinische Studie* was translated in 1899. Furthermore, two Japanese sexologists, (Ryuzaburo Takebe and Minosuke Kimura, who took a keen interest in western sexology) published their collaborative work on sexual life: *Danjo Kogotokushitsu Mondo* (*A Dialogue between Man and Woman on the Characteristics of Sexual Intercourse*) in 1886 (for the details of these works see Saito 5–8). All these sexological works, which were widely read, encouraged their readers to appreciate sexual life or explained sexual abnormalities in detail from a scientific point of view. The western interest in sexuality was later developed by Sigmund Freud, who published *Die Traumdeutung* in 1900. Lawrence later encountered his theory through Frieda and criticized it in *Fantasia of the Unconscious.*

When Akiko discussed the problem of marriage and sexual desire in her 1917 essay 'A Question about the Morality between Man and Woman' she referred to sexologists:

According to some doctors' theories, unfulfilled heterosexual love relations are often said to result from unsatisfied sexual desire in married life, and opinion leaders on the morality of man and woman have disregarded this important matter. (Yosano, *Collected Works* 16: 431 (my translation); see also the 1922 essay 'Education of Sex', *Collected Works* 18: 413–14)

Akiko is probably referring to the sexologists mentioned above. Their works had been published long before this essay and she must have read them much earlier, because she was an avid reader not only of various kinds of classic and modern Japanese books and literary journals but also of western 'translations' (H. Sato, *Akiko Mandala* 36).

With this background before her literary debut, the 24-year-old woman poet Akiko Hou's (later Akiko Yosano's) *Tangled Hair* (1901) shocked oppressive Confucian morality. It was a daring proclamation of sensuality and sexuality, based upon her own passionate love for her 28-year-old future husband (Odagiri 1–2; Noda 135). They fell in love in the summer of 1900 when Tekkan, poet and editor of *Morning Star*, went from Tokyo to Osaka to attend a literary circle of which Akiko was a member. He eventually took her as his new wife, abandoning his former wife and child.

His decision to marry Akiko in 1901 was a bit similar to Frieda Weekley's choosing Lawrence in 1912 as her new husband, rejecting Ernest Weekley: Akiko resembles Lawrence in daring to leave her home (and deeply-opposed family) in Osaka, to live with Tekkan in Tokyo. Akiko, like Lawrence, was so passionate that she finally won the heart of Tekkan (just as Lawrence did Frieda's).

Despite the western and Japanese sexologists' scientific books, *Tangled Hair* opened a new frontier of spontaneous sensuality and sexuality. Japanese literary milieux, dominated by Confucian morality, had witnessed no such flaming passion as Akiko's. Lawrence's *Look! We Have Come Through!* was a similarly new celebration in English of marriage, and of spontaneous sensuality and sexuality; an entirely new voice in late-Edwardian morality.

To compare the expression of sensuality and sexuality in the two books, consider first Akiko's four Tanka poems:

(1)   Aren't you sad,
        only arguing about the way of life?
        Aren't you sad,
        Never touching my soft warm body
        which is full of passionate blood? (Noda (ed.),
        Tangled Hair 8) (my translation)[4]

To Akiko, touch is essential between man and woman, or husband and wife. Without touch life is barren.

(2)   Spring is short.
        Is there any other immortal life but our passionate life?
        I've induced him to touch my breasts
        which are full of vital life. (Noda (ed.), *Tangled Hair* 43)

Physical touch matters most when she marries.

(3)   So much aching is my heart
        from thinking of you, my godly love
        who treads on the lily,
        I'd like to offer my bare breasts
        To you, my dear. (Noda (ed.), *Tangled Hair* 10)

Akiko tries to ease her aching heart by offering her bare breasts to her lover and wants to be embraced by him.

(4)   Pressing the breasts,
        I have softly kicked the veil of mystery.
        How crimson is the flower here! (Noda (ed.),
            Tangled Hair 13)

One commentary on this poem says that 'it symbolically suggests (with the visual imagery, as in a nude painting) Akiko's first sexual intercourse and fulfilment' with her lover (Satake 80; see also *The Poetry of Japan* vol. 4: 113; Goldstein and Shinoda, 'Notes' 130). In her recent study of Akiko Yosano Beichman relates this poem to Titian's painting 'The Penitence of Mary Magdalene', which Akiko must have seen 'in her and Tekkan's own home' (219)[5]: Mary Magdalene, her hand pressed to her breast in emotion, clarifies the gesture of the speaker (of Akiko's poem) in 'Pressing her breast' (Chibusa osae)' (218). The painting and the poem, Beichman argues, cast a 'mutual reflection' (218). However, unlike the penitent Mary Magdalene (who denies sexual desires and aspires towards God in pressing her breast) Akiko, in pressing her breasts, affirms sexual desire and attains fulfilment. In this sense 'Akiko's poem is about the erotic subtext of Titian's painting, the pagan sensuality beneath his Christian spirituality' (Beichman 185). Akiko's sensuality is very Lawrentian. In 1909 Lawrence saw some of Titian's paintings in the Dulwich art gallery (L i 124), and he later valued Titian's 'gleam of the warm procreative body' in 'Introduction to These Paintings' (LEA 194) or made Connie comment on Titian's 'nude women' in The First Lady Chatterley: 'I one day suddenly felt, in all my body, the soft glowing loveliness, loveliness of the flesh – then I said to myself, quite distinct and alone, "that is the immortality of the flesh"' (FSLC 50).

In each of Akiko's Tanka poems physical or sexual imagery is evident or implied, and it is said that Tangled Hair had a revolutionary impact on many Japanese readers when it was first published. Likewise, Lawrence's poems in Look! We Have Come Through! (1917) presented stunning sensual and sexual imagery. In 'Song of a Man Who Is Loved', for example, Lawrence describes breasts as 'a tower of strength':

Between her breasts is my home, between her breasts.
Three sides set on me space and fear, but the fourth side rests
Sure and a tower of strength, 'twixt the walls of her breasts.
(Poems 203)

Lawrence says in 'Manifesto' that his 'hunger for the woman' which is 'very deep, and ravening' (Poems 217), was appeased at last, again 'between her breasts':

This comes right at last.
When a man is rich (with the woman's body at his side), he loses at last the hunger fear,
I lost at last the fierceness that fears it will starve.
I could put my face at last between her breasts
and know that they were given for ever
that I should never starve,
never perish;

I had eaten of the bread that satisfies
and my body's body was appeased,
there was peace and richness,
fulfilment. (*Poems* 217–18)

Just as Akiko's breasts were a spring of life for her to nurture physically-based love between her and her husband, Frieda's breasts for Lawrence were 'a haven of peace' (*Poems* 204) putting his heart into deeper rest ('my still heart (is) full of security') (*Poems* 204).

Most significantly, for Lawrence and Akiko, sexual intercourse is the doorway to a deeper life-mystery. Akiko says: 'I have softly kicked the veil of mystery', suggesting she experiences life-mystery through sexual intercourse. Lawrence too found life-mystery in 'New Heaven and Earth':

I touched her flank and knew I was carried by the current in death
over to the new world (...) (*Poems* 213)

And he concludes this poem with his discovery of 'the sources of mystery':

The unknown, strong current of life supreme
drowns me and sweeps me away and holds me down
to the sources of mystery, in the depths (...) (*Poems* 214)

Thus, for Lawrence and Akiko, sexuality is not sexuality alone: rather it is a springboard from which to leap into the source of life-mystery, the human body.

Creating a new frontier of sensuality and sexuality Akiko is a forerunner of the modern Japanese literature of passionate heterosexual love, and Lawrence is her English counterpart. Both challenged social taboo by becoming involved with a married man or woman whom they loved passionately and thereby gained, for themselves and their partners, a new life and fulfilment. Above all, fighting against every accusation, both succeeded in writing great poetry.

iii

One big difference between Lawrence and Akiko, however, is that he wrote many novels and is recognized as one of the greatest novelists of 20th-century England, whereas she is esteemed more as a poet than a novelist (though she did write a few novels). Another difference is that Lawrence never fathered a child and did not experience child-rearing, whereas Akiko had 11 children and pursued her literary career in the midst of very difficult child-rearing, despite the help of a housemaid and her husband. However, both Lawrence and Akiko valued warm touch with a child (as well as marriage and family life). Akiko defended motherhood from her own experience of child-rearing and distanced herself from the flourishing blue-stocking ideologues who (like their western counterparts in demanding women's individual freedom from their subjugated status) denigrated child-rearing and motherhood within the marital partnership.

Akiko loved physical touch with her child, as did Lawrence too, though he did not have a child. Even before her marriage Akiko wrote an imaginative poem about bearing a child, 'Haha Gokoro' ('Motherly Love'),[6] in which she proclaimed that she would like to rear the child herself with its physical beauty:

> It is far more interesting to rear my own baby
> Than to have a canary's chick as a pet.
> The chick's down is shabby,
> Its footing weak.
> My heart is encouraged and strengthened
> To see the white naked soft body of the baby
> Bathing in a tub.
> Exactly like your parents' are,
> My dear baby,
> Your limbs and trunk and complexion.
> So far dearer to me you are, my dear,
> Than the canary's chick, the different species. (*Selected Poems* 22–3)

Even in this poem Akiko enjoys her soft touching with the baby and is determined to rear it with her own hands. And when she did have a baby she found a greater joy in the movements of Auguste than in her

121

own literary achievement. The baby was named after the French sculptor Auguste Rodin, whom she met in Paris in 1912:[7]

> Auguste, Auguste,
> My dear five-year-old baby Auguste
> You are truly a representative of 'truth'.
> How can I put into my own words
> Even one of your natural movements
> When you spread your hands?
> All I can do is just look at you
> In wonder.
>
> … … … .
>
> How can my simple literary art
> Excel and compete with your being? ('Auguste') (1917) (*Selected Poems* 21)

The young Lawrence also loved the soft touch of a child, probably while he played in the grass with Hilda Mary Jones (the second daughter of John William and Marie Jones, at whose house Lawrence lodged while he was teaching at Croydon) (*Poems* 841). In 'Baby Running Barefoot' Lawrence imagines feeling the baby's feet with his hands:

> And I wish that the baby would tack across here to me
> Like a wind-shadow running on a pond, so she could stand
> With two little bare white feet upon my knee
> And I could feel her feet in either hand
>
> Cool as syringa buds in morning hours,
> Or firm and silken as young peony flowers. (*Poems* 33)

The flower similes intensify the softness of the child's feet. In another poem, 'A Baby Asleep after Pain' Lawrence is surprised to find that the lightweight body of a baby before it sleeps is now 'a heaviness' and 'a weariness' (*Poems* 41) while it is sleeping. This is another example of Lawrence's physical or bodily understanding, rejecting any idealistic abstraction. Just as Akiko in 'Motherly Love' bathes her baby and touches its soft body with her hands, so Lawrence in 'Baby Running Barefoot' wants to enjoy the soft feet of the child with his hands while he is playing with her in the grass. In both cases the hands are a channel connecting the two lives, the adult's and the child's. In both poems physicality is dominant; both reject any idealistic abstraction. For Lawrence and Akiko contact with the child puts them into a vivid flow of warm life. Akiko would agree with Lawrence that:

> We don't exist unless we are deeply and sensually in touch
> with that which can be touched but not known. ('Non-existence',
> *Poems* 528)

Lawrence's and Akiko's vivid sense of life-flow in human touch was lacking in the feminist ideologies, which seemed too abstract and idealistic. While Akiko values most the man and woman relationship based on physical contact and also child-rearing Lawrence values the man and woman relationship as the star-equilibrium' beautifully expressed in *Women in Love* (319). All human relationship should be based on touch, as he stated in his poem 'Non-existence'.

While Akiko insisted that motherhood and child-rearing should be matters for individual women or families to decide the social reformer Raicho Hiratsuka (1886–1971), one of the leading blue-stocking ideologues following western models, considered (after having a child with her lover Hiroshi Okuno in 1915) that motherhood and child-rearing should be supported by the state because women contribute to the state and mankind by bearing children (Hiratsuka, *Selected Works* 2:353; Kobayashi, 'Introduction', 370).

Skeptical of the blue-stocking ideologues' popular idea of the state support for motherhood and child-rearing Akiko, in the 1918 essays 'My Skirmish with Mrs. Hiratsuka' and 'My Reply to Mrs. Hiratsuka, Mrs.Yamada, and Mrs. Yamakawa' (*Critical Essays* 203–06; 232–5), criticized them for being too dependent on the state in individual matters and for underestimating the value of individual freedom and the spirit of independence in an individual family. Their quarrels are well-known in the history of Japanese women's studies as the 'Disputes over Motherhood Support'. Akiko, as a poet, emphasized women's independence and the development of their creative abilities while Hiratsuka, as a social reformer, emphasized social mobility for the sake of women's liberation.

Hiratsuka's demand for state support of motherhood echoes the early 20th-century English women's suffrage movement, which also argued for 'state welfare for mothers' (Notes to *WP* 393). This is reflected in Lawrence's *The White Peacock*: after becoming a socialist, George Saxton 'hold(s) forth about the state endowment of mothers' (296) along the lines of women suffragettes and the Fabian Society. In the same novel Lettie, after her marriage with Leslie, has few aims in her life and is characterized as a woman who 'escape(s)' 'the responsibilities of her own development' (284). Akiko and Lawrence both accord most value to women's individual self-development.

As for family values Lawrence considers, like Akiko, that the family is an important social unit independent of state intervention. While Akiko (who was not a Christian) naturally does not consider the social importance of marriage and family from a Christian point of view, at the end of his life Lawrence does. He recognizes in 'A Propos of *Lady Chatterley's Lover*' that 'perhaps the greatest contribution to the social life of man made by Christianity is – marriage' (*LCL* 321). He goes on to indicate its social significance in the state:

> Christianity established the little autonomy of the family within the greater rule of the State. Christianity made marriage in some respects inviolate, not to be violated by the State. It is marriage, perhaps, which has given man the best of his freedom, given him his little kingdom of his own within the big kingdom of the State, given him his foothold of independence on which to stand and resist an unjust State. Man and wife, a king and a queen with one or two subjects, and a few square yards of territory of their own: this, really, is marriage. (321)

Admittedly, Lawrence's ideas about marriage and the family were complicated, for as a great individualist he feared the constricting effect of social institutions. Still, he always believed in marriage. To Lawrence, the family was a little independent 'kingdom' with a king, a queen and a few subjects within 'the big kingdom of the State'.

Lawrence and Akiko were both exponents of freedom from state intervention in family matters, because they believed that the family is the most important basis of society. In Lawrence's words marriage, or family life, is 'a true freedom because it is a true fulfilment for man, woman and children' ('A Propos', *LCL* 321). Akiko was the joint creator of a family of 11 children.

iv

A third common feature of Lawrence and Akiko is that they were tree-worshippers, sun-worshippers and cosmic life believers, with a strong tie with nature. Lawrence's tree worship, as is seen in the previous chapter, is most manifest in *Fantasia of the Unconscious* (1921). In the Black Forest in Germany, he felt the tree-power of the forest enabling him to write: he says that the tree has a 'huge, plunging, tremendous soul (…) Now I like it, I worship it', though he 'used to be afraid' (*FU* 86–7).

In New Mexico in 1924, he wrote:('the) tree has its own aura of life (…) And the tree is still within the allness of Pan' (*MM* 158). The 1925 essay 'Aristocracy' also shows his tree worship: he says that 'in so far as he (the tree) is a vast, powerful, silent life, you should worship him' (*RDP* 372).

Just as Lawrence intuits the vital life of trees and has a profound sense of awe toward them, Akiko also senses their life power as in her poem 'Mori no Taiju' ('The Giant Tree of the Forest') (1915):

> Oh, Giant of the forest,
> One-thousand-year old tree,
> Standing in front of you,
> I am a humble nature worshipper.
>
> … … … .
> Oh, one-thousand-year-old tree,
> I, only a human of ephemeral life,
> How encouraged and strengthened I am by you!
> I ponder on you, stepping upon your shadow,
> I am singing of you, embracing your trunk.
> I wish, after I died, I were buried at the foot of you,
> And would continue to offer my insatiable love to you,

In the underground,
Sipping your pure salve and passionate hidden tears.
(*Selected Poems* 50–2)

Akiko's worship of the giant tree (like Morisaki's, which we have seen in chapter 9) is exactly like Lawrence's and the soul's intermingling with tree life, whether after death (in Akiko's case) or during life (in Lawrence's case) is similar.

Lawrence expresses sun worship, most clearly in the short story 'Sun' and in *Apocalypse*. In 'Sun' the heroine, Juliet, suffers from a mental disorder in New York. After she travels to an island in the Mediterranean she recuperates in the sunshine, feeling the warm rays of the sun penetrating her womb:

> Something deep inside her unfolded and relaxed, and she was given to a cosmic influence. By some mysterious will inside her, deeper than her known consciousness and her known will, she was put into connection with the sun, and the stream of the sun flowed through her, round her womb. (*WWRA* 26)

While 'Sun' is a short story about Juliet's individual recuperation, in *Apocalypse* Lawrence discusses the modern problem of human disconnectedness and the way of overcoming it from a wider perspective. He advocates the establishment of a living relationship with the sun accompanied by its worship:

> When I hear modern people complain of being lonely then I know what has happened. They have lost the cosmos. – It is nothing human and personal that we are short of. What we lack is cosmic life, the sun in us and the moon in us. We can't get the sun in us by lying naked like pigs on a beach. The very sun that is bronzing us is inwardly disintegrating us. (…) We can only get the sun by a sort of worship: and the same the moon. By *going forth* to worship the sun, worship that is felt in the blood. Tricks and postures only make matters worse. (*A* 78) (Lawrence's italics)

When she bore a child, Akiko wrote a poem of joy at childbirth: 'Sanshitsu no Yoake' ('Daybreak in the Maternity Room') (1914). Although exhausted by hard labour, she writes:

> Yet, my new emotion is
> Like a sun-worshipper's belief.
> Receive my raised hands,
> Oh, Sun, Queen of Dawn.
>
> Oh, Sun, you too have had troubles of night and winter.
> Millions of million times since time immemorial,
> You have rejuvenated yourself by going through the pains of
>   death.
> How powerful are the flames of heaven!
> I still follow you,
> Oh, Sun. (*Selected Poems* 22–3)

Akiko's sun worship is expanded into her belief in cosmic life. In 'Natsu no Chikara' ('The Power of Summer') (1924) she is in deep connection with cosmic life:

> I live, most energetically,
> Wiping sweat after sweat, with a pen in my hand.
> Now, I am fully electrified by cosmic life,
> Finding myself being filled with ecstasy.
>   … … …
> Summer is flaming up with me. (*Selected Poems* 76)

Akiko feels life-mystery in trees, sun, and sexuality. Haruo Sato, one of the most important Japanese novelists of the 20th century and the author of a novel about Akiko (*Akiko Mandala)* commented that 'she found and wrote her poetry when she felt the pulsating life in everything in the universe' (Sato, 'Introduction' 208: my translation). Her sense of life is very Lawrentian, with the same sense of throbbing life as is demonstrated in such poems as 'The Wild Common', 'A Man Who Died', 'Corot', 'Renascence' and 'Craving for Spring'.

In conclusion, Lawrence and Akiko are poets of human touch and cosmic life who sought to establish a vital contact between human beings and with nature. They warned against ideological extremity and rigid morality. Without knowing each other, they shared the new evaluation of sexuality in the west and in Japan. Their similar beliefs help explain why the very English writer Lawrence is easily approached by many Japanese readers.

Lawrence wrote to Mary Cannan from Italy in July 1921 telling her that 'Insole writes from Japan that it is perfectly fascinating. I should like to see it – also Siam. Something more velvety than Europe' (*L* iv 49). If Lawrence had visited Japan when he travelled to Ceylon and Australia in 1922 he might have met the well-known Japanese woman poet Akiko Yosano in Tokyo, just as she had met the French sculptor Auguste Rodin (1840–1917) in Paris in 1912. And then Lawrence and Akiko might have exchanged opinions and letters, which would surely benefit us now. But that intriguing possibility never happened.

Notes

1. There was a social change in the world of painting as well before Akiko's *Tangled Hair* was published in 1901: Kuroda Seiki, 'who had lived in France for several years and studied painting with Raphaël Collin in Paris', became a pioneer painter of a nude portrait of a woman called 'Chosho' ('Morning Toilette') in Japan. Its exhibition in 1895 (Beichman 202) caused an uproar.
2. See Hungarian designer P. Horter's art nouveau design in No. 13 (1901), p. 16.
3. All these sketches or paintings were added to each issue of the journal as a separate supplement of good quality printing.
4. Hereafter the translations of every poem of Akiko in this paper, unless otherwise stated, are all mine.
5. Beside 'The Penitence of Mary Magdalene' Akiko must have seen Titian's 'Venus Anadyomene' and 'Venus and Cupid' (Beichman 218–19), and she wrote a poem about his work: 'Against the shabby wall / Titian's glory pains me / On such a night / hide not / our brimming sake jug' (Noda (ed.), *Tangled Hair* 30) (translated by Beichman 218). For Titian's paintings see 'Olga's Gallery' <http://www.abcgallery.com/T/titian/titian > (31 August 2003).

6. Akiko wrote this poem in 1901, as is indicated at the end of the poem: therefore, as Osamu Nishigaki points out ('Note for Appreciation' 185), Akiko had no child at this time. It was first published in 1909 (Yosano, *Collected Works* 9:108).
7. Akiko wrote an essay called 'Rodan Ou ni Atta Hi' ('The Day When I Met Old Rodin'), in which she says she was deeply impressed by his great loving heart (Yosano, *Collected Works* 15: 340).

CHAPTER 11

D. H. LAWRENCE AND SEI ITO: CHARACTERISTICS OF THE SEXUAL SCENES IN THEIR NOVELS

i

One of the leading Lawrence scholars in Japan, Takaji Shibata, has published two books on comparative literature dealing with D. H. Lawrence and other writers: one of them is *D. H. Lawrence and Hideo Kobayashi* (1989), in which Shibata compares Lawrence the novelist as a priest of love with Kobayashi the literary critic as a priest of life. The two writers are both fully discussed as serious writers in their lives.

In 1991 Shibata published another book on comparative literature: *Joyce, Lawrence and Sei Ito*, dealing with the three novelists. His comparison of the novelists makes good sense because Ito was a serious reader not only of D. H. Lawrence but also of James Joyce. Ito translated many of Lawrence's works from the 1930s to the 1960s as well as Joyce's *Ulysses* in 1931 and 1934. Although Shibata makes a first and interesting attempt to compare the three novelists it is a pity that he juxtaposes their works mainly to point out their similarities, rather than to elucidate their essential differences. In this chapter I will take up Lawrence and Ito here to make a contribution to Lawrentian scholarship and to compare them by examining the treatment of sex, which the two novelists are much interested in and which Shibata does not fully examine in his book.

Sei Ito (1905–1969) was a prolific writer like Lawrence: the *Collected Works* of Ito's novels, essays and poems consist of 24 volumes published by Shincho-sha Press, Tokyo, in 1972. He was active as a translator, too. He translated Lawrence's four novels: *Lady Chatterley's Lover* in 1935, 1936, and 1950, *St. Mawr* in 1937, *Sons and Lovers* in 1960, *Women in Love* in 1963, Lawrence's letters in 1956, many of his essays in 1936 and 1937 and he edited and translated an anthology of selected passages of

Lawrence's works in 1937.[1] Among the Japanese novelists Ito was the most enthusiastic reader of Lawrence. How, then, does Ito accept or make use of Lawrence's works or philosophy and create his own unique literary world in his novels? To answer this question I will deal with Ito's three novels: *Kouzui* (*The Flood*) (1956–8), *Hakkutsu* (*Excavations*) (1962–4) and his last work *Henyou* (*Transformations*) (1967–8)[2] (in each of which he describes sexual scenes) and Lawrence's novel *Lady Chatterley's Lover.* I will then compare them to see how much Ito owes to Lawrence and how essentially different the two novelists are, despite Ito's continued efforts to introduce Lawrence to Japanese readers.

ii

In *Excavations*, *The Flood* and *Transformations* Ito deals with sex to show how a husband is strongly urged by sexual desire towards love affairs with another woman, or his wife with another man. They are always on the point of breaking the family tie, which will be kept in the end. In *Excavations* the hero, Keizo Tsuchitani (professor of Japanese literature), wants to meet Kumeko Torii (assistant professor of Japanese literature at a different university) without being detected by his wife. Keizo and Kumeko only find sensual satisfaction when they meet secretly: they see sex only as an instrument of physical satisfaction and are indifferent to their humanity. One day when they meet in a hotel and have sexual contact Keizo asks Kumeko to forget him (as if he were a stranger to her) after the rendezvous is over, because he has no intention to further develop their relationship: he is afraid that the affair will be known to his wife. Yet he is tempted to meet Kumeko again, for he cannot overcome his strong sexual desire towards her. He uses Kumeko to satisfy his own desire, but does not care for her. He is egocentric and, lacking gentleness, is insensitive to her. Kumeko, on the other hand, detects his fear of the affair and despises him and begins to be arrogant towards him during their physical contact:

> There was a mixed feeling of hate and arrogance in the eyes of Kumeko. Keizo could not endure her look of hate. When he lost his will to control himself, his desire urged him to make love again. He saw Kumeko's body and touched her while she lay before him. Then he began to force himself upon her again.

> Kumeko, too, began to seek satisfaction and cried. Keizo knew
> she had carnal passion, as if it gushed out. (*Excavations* 165)[3]

Keizo, however, finds it useless and hopeless to continue his advances when he knows the mechanical aspect of her actions and the insensitivity of his actions:

> When Kumeko's actions became mechanical, Keizo suddenly
> realized how barren her actions were and how insensitive he
> was when he forced her to continue to act. Then he could not
> go on any longer and gave up, being fed up with excitement.
> (165–6)

Keizo and Kumeko take only physical action to gain sensual satisfaction without any heart-to-heart communications.

This reminds us of Michaelis' behaviour towards Connie in *Lady Chatterley's Lover*. When Connie notices that her husband Clifford is cold-hearted to everybody she turns away from him, first to Michaelis – a thirty-year-old dramatist – and then to Mellors, a gamekeeper on the Chatterley estate. Though Michaelis is young he looks 'endlessly old', and is filled with 'fathomless disillusion' (23). He has no hope to live except for a desire for success in the world and takes no responsibility as a citizen. He is called an 'antisocial' 'outsider' (28) and he is a victim of utter loneliness, having no living connection with anybody. Connie, without realizing his cold-heartedness, comes to love him and has sexual contact with him several times. When she almost wants to get married to him, being deceived by his kind words, he changes his mind suddenly and detaches himself from her. He discourages her in their intercourse:

> He was a more excited lover that night, with his strange, small
> boy's excitement and his small boy's frail nakedness. Connie
> found it impossible to come to her crisis before he had really
> finished his. And he roused a certain craving passion in her,
> with his little boy's nakedness and softness, she had to go on
> after he had finished, in the wild tumult and heaving of her
> loins, while he heroically kept himself up and present in her,

with all his will and self-offering, till she brought about her own wild crisis, with weird little cries. (53)

Lawrence here presents Michaelis as a man who has no sympathy with Connie. He is too egoistic a man. And in fact, it is shown to the reader in the following passage that he is such an insensitive person:

'You keep on for hours after I've gone off – and I have to hang on with my teeth till you bring yourself off, by your own exertions.'

She was stunned by this unexpected piece of brutality, at that moment when she was glowing with a sort of pleasure beyond words, and a sort of love of him. (54)

Michaelis is a self-centred fellow who does not care how Connie will feel when she hears these unfeeling words. During the 1951 Chatterley trial, Sei Ito read a defending essay called 'Characteristics of the Sexual Scenes in *Lady Chatterley's Lover*', and, as he points out in this essay (640–2), Lawrence creates Michaelis as one whose egoism is reflected in his sexual behaviour. Just as Michaelis is egocentric and insensitive in his sexual behaviour, so are Keizo and Kumeko in theirs. Ito sees sex, as Lawrence and does, as a place where one's sense of humanity is revealed. In *Excavations* Ito uses sex to show the egoism of a modern man or woman such as Keizo orKumeko and to emphasize their sense of loneliness as Lawrence emphasizes Michaelis's loneliness in *Lady Chatterley's Lover*. Keizo and Kumeko are, like Michaelis, doomed to be lonely because neither of them wants to establish a warm human relationship.

The same theme is dealt with in another novel, *The Flood*, and in a different way. In this novel Ito intensifies man's egoism and sense of loneliness by presenting four main characters who seek sexual satisfaction: Sahei Sanada, a successful engineer; his wife Fumiko; their daughter Takako, who is a university student; and Shoukichi Kuga, Sanada's friend and professor of engineering. All of them have lovers. Sanada wants to renew the old relationship with his lover Sachiko Nishiyama, and meets her several times. Sachiko would like to get married to him but finally breaks away from him, because Sanada has no intention of getting divorced from his wife. He only would like to keep her as his lover: this is his egoism, which does not satisfy her earnest wish.

While Sanada has a love affair with Sachiko his wife Fumiko is also tempted to have an affair, and meets her daughter's piano instructor Itazaki secretly. Thus the husband and wife deceive each other, yet keep on living together as if nothing wrong happened. As long as their affairs are kept secret their excitements are intensified. Yet they are on the point of breaking their marital relationships, and feel lonelier and lonelier because they know they are deceiving their partners. While Sanada and his wife have love affairs separately their daughter Takako has dates with her boyfriend, an ambitious young university assistant (Kyosuke Tanemura) who would like to make advances in the world by obtaining favours of Takako's father – who has succeeded in his business as an engineer. The young man's ambition drives him to seduce her to make her his wife by force. Though there is little love between them she thinks it better to get married to him soon: her parents agree with her and hastily marry them, pretending to arrange everything in good order because the parents do not like to make their daughter's forced marriage a public matter. When the wedding celebration party is held the parents and the daughter pretend to love the young man, but they know well that they do not love him. Sanada is now a rich man, for he has invented a new chemical which brings a lot of profit to his company: he is, in return, rewarded with a higher salary and is promoted to a higher post. The family becomes financially rich, with many newly-bought things at home coming in as if in a flood: they are materially satisfied, yet they are spiritually very poor. For them sex also remains on the material level, having no spiritual meaning. Ito thus characterizes the superficiality of the rich family.

Shoukichi Kuga (Sanada's friend and professor of engineering) is also characterized as superficial, for he is obsessed with love affairs and money. He is a boss in his academic society of engineering and knows that Sanada wants to obtain an engineering doctorate. Kuga suggests that Sanada submit a dissertation to Kuga's university, where he will be an examiner of the dissertation. The professor does not demand any money from his now-rich friend in return: he merely hints to him that he is in trouble in continuing a love affair with his lover and is in need of money. Kuga's real intention is to extort money from this rich engineer, who instantly understands what the professor means by hinting like that and gets the money ready for him. The money works so well that the degree is granted to Sanada. Thus, money decides everything between the professor and the degree candidate and between the professor and his lover. These are dreary human situations which Ito describes in detail with a realist's eyes. The barrenness of their life is quite close to that of Gerald Crich in *Women in Love:* Gerald acutely feels the meaninglessness of his life after he completes the mechanization of his mines and miners for the sake of his profits.

The Flood, therefore, does not give the reader any Lawrentian hope in life. Ito's last novel – *Transformations* – however, shows something Lawrentian. Here Ito creates a unique world of one man and three women and seems to come close to Lawrence's idea of man and woman for the first time, though the two novelists are essentially different. Hokumei Tatsuta (the hero of this novel), a painter of Japanese paintings, is nearly 60 years old and has three lovers: Utako Kobuchi, Sakiko Maeyama and Senko Kouno. While in the two novels *Excavations* and *The Flood* the men consider marriage to be a prison from which they want to get free (and they want to enjoy themselves with their mistresses) Tatsuta in *Transformations* is freed from his marriage bond, for in his forties his wife died and now he is a widower. After her death the three women, Utako, Sakiko and Senko play important roles in his life.

Utako – a barmaid – was once Tatsuta's mistress when she was in her twenties and he in his forties. At that time when she was sexually united with him she did not end up only with physical sensations: she showed delicate and refined feelings towards him. But when they meet again 20 years later she has no such feelings, and is nothing but a fellow of carnal satisfaction. She is, Ito describes, 'like a wild bird which seeks a prey' (*Transformations* 508). Tastuta does not like her as an individual woman now yet he is attracted to her only for his sexual desire. For his strong sexuality is, Ito says, 'inborn' (398).

Compared with Utako, Sakiko and Senko are Tatsuta's and perhaps Ito's ideal women, because they have a balance of sexuality and intellectuality. Sakiko is a master of Japanese dancing and is now just over 60 years old. She is a sister of Mansaku Kurata, Tatsuta's close friend. When Kurata and Tatsuta are university students, they spend one night at Sakiko's house. She is then a married woman but is ill-treated by her husband

and she wants to meet a gentle-hearted man like Tatsuta. She secretly creeps into Tatsuta's room and sleeps with him while he is sleeping. She just wants a warm touch of him, which heals her ill-bruised heart (this is really Lawrentian). Tatsuta, though being awakened, lets her do as she pleases without taking any action on his part. She does it only once that night, and on the following morning neither of them mentions the touch. She does not see him again for nearly 40 years after that.

Sakiko's brother, Mansaku Kurata, achieves fame as a novelist and dies at the age of 59. After his death a memorial to him is erected in his home town, where his friend Tatsuta goes to attend the unveiling ceremony. There he meets Sakiko, now a widow, after 40 years' separation. When the ceremony is over Tatsuta is invited to Sakiko's house. She recollects her past, while they lie together in bed. She explains why she crept into his bed 40 years ago: she was lonely and needed a warm physical touch to heal her loneliness. Now Sakiko and Tatsuta are free to act and want to fulfil sexual desires. At this moment he notices that she is not only driven by sexual impulse but behaves herself elegantly, with a well-controlled mind:

> It is almost an art itself how Sakiko is intoxicated with his embrace while she is recollecting her past. Dancing is an art to express physical actions in harmony with the mind. Sakiko keeps that sense of harmony of body and mind in her sexual behaviour and in readjusting herself to her everyday life as well after their intercourse is over. (531)

Tatsuta discovers that Sakiko's sexual life is well controlled by her artistic sense of dancing, and she has a beautiful balance between her physical life and intellectual life. Again they have this experience on only one night, but it is a significant occasion for him to find a good example of that balance. A few weeks after he goes back home she dies suddenly, expressing her gratitude for his companionship.

Before Tatsuta sees Sakiko at the unveiling ceremony he has a love affair with another woman, Senko, who is also just over 60 years old and still active as a poetess. She is a widow, too. Tatsuta happens to meet her at an art gallery, makes friends with her and has a love affair with her. She is full of vitality when she is sexually united with him: her sex has, Ito says, 'the power of a thunder goddess' (407). And at the same time she, as a poetess, is so highly cultured that she does not lose her self-possession:

> Though she has been driven by impulses to fulfil her desires with him, she recovers herself soon after everything is finished and resumes her behaviour as poetess without losing her composure. (531)

Tatsuta thinks that since she always thinks about the meaning of life as a poetess, she regards sex as an essential part of human life. And he goes on to reflect himself:

> Isn't it true that one can grasp the true joy of sex only when one grasps the meaning of human life? Isn't it also true that if a woman like Senko has rich and refined sensibility and personality and can enjoy her sexual life, then she has real sex, and that if she fulfils herself in her sexual contact with a man spontaneously in spite of her restraining will or hesitation, then her joy is most human? (532)

In other words, Tatsuta realizes that unless one is well cultured and has refined sensibility, one's sex will lose its true meaning: the physical and the mental, therefore (he considers) must be interrelated. His realization is quite Lawrentian.

In Lawrence's novels like *Women in Love* or *Lady Chatterley's Lover* he tries to balance the physical with the mental or, to use Lawrentian terms, to balance 'blood consciousness' with 'mental consciousness' (*L* ii 470). The well-known concept of 'star-equilibrium' in *Women in Love* not only means the balance between Birkin and Ursula or between man and woman but also suggests the balance between the physical and the mental, because without the latter balance man and woman cannot be whole beings and achieve equilibrium between themselves. The marriage between Connie and Mellors, which is based on tenderness in *Lady Chatterley's Lover,* is another example of that balance. Especially in the case of Connie, her mental self is to be harmonized with her sensual self through her contact with Mellors. Ito seems to incorporate the Lawrentian philosophy of balance between body and mind in his last novel, *Transformations*.

It should be noted, however, that there are essential differences between Ito and Lawrence. While Lawrence always thinks about the true meaning of marriage between one man and one woman both in the physical and mental sense, Ito does not necessarily do so. What matters most to Ito is a natural flow of feeling rather than a moral principle in marriage. In principle Ito defends the present system of monogamy, because he thinks that without it family structures would be broken and social disorder would be caused. Yet, in reality, he has a strong wish that man's inborn impulses – including sexual ones – would be admitted fully without worrying about marital obligations (Ito, *Twelve Chapters* 129, 132–33). This strong wish is most manifestly realized in Tatsuta, Sakiko and Senko. Tatsuta enjoys most the meetings with Sakiko and Senko at respective instances. He neither binds himself to one of these women nor wants to get married to either of them. Neither do the women. They also enjoy their individual life without any moral obligation now that they are widows and are at an older age. Lawrence's idea of marriage is basically of Christian morality, while Ito's is not. Ito's idea is not so much moralistic as aesthetic. Therefore, Ito's characters in his novels do not try to create a marital relationship (which Lawrence's characters do). In this sense Ito stands at a different position from Lawrence.

The difference is perhaps the difference between Christian morality and traditional Japanese aesthetics. Christianity demands strict morality in marriage, whereas exponents of Japanese aesthetics value a natural flow of life most: for this reason the sense of morality is not so strictly demanded in a Japanese society as in a Christian society. Tatsuta, Sakiko and Senko have no intention to marry again after they lose their spouses. All they want to do is to enjoy, as widower or widow, a spontaneous sexual life without bothering about moral restrictions as long as old age permits them to: though they follow sexual impulses they are not promiscuous, because they try to enjoy the best moments of their old lives only with their trusted and cultured friend. Since exponents of Japanese aesthetics praise a natural flow of life, including sexuality, their appraisal of sexuality as an essential part of their life is considered to be a traditional Japanese characteristic: this goes back to the 9th-century novel *The Tale of Genji*, by Lady Murasaki, in which the tender-hearted hero Genji loves many attractive women though suffering, too, because of his love affairs).

It is not until Ito makes his characters of old age a widower or widows in *Transformations* that he can create them as free and fulfilled individuals and let them follow their spontaneous sexuality. Such characters cannot be seen in any of Lawrence's works.[4] They are Ito's most unique creations and contributions to Japanese literature, in which he finally succeeds in his last novel (which has been considered to be 'one of the greatest novels in modern Japanese literature as well as the best of his novels') (Hirano 143).

There is another difference between Lawrence and Ito to be mentioned. While in Lawrence's works, whether in *Lady Chatterley's Lover* or *Women in Love*, the life-force of nature is essential and vital or sacred for the inner transformations or healing processes of heroes or heroines to take place. In Ito's three novels nature is not given any important meaning for his characters, which is entirely an un-Lawrentian consequence (despite Ito's earnest commitment to Lawrence's novels, which are full of fascinating natural descriptions). It is because Ito places his characters in a big city which lacks nature, not in such a rural area or forest as where Lawrence places his characters. It should be noticed, however, as Chiseki Asahi indicates (Asahi 49) that in his early works (such as *Yukiakari no Michi* (*The Snow-lit Road*) and *Seibutsusai* (*The Festival of Living Creatures*)) Ito depicts nature as vital life like Lawrence does. But Ito does not further develop that sense of nature in his later novels, as we have seen.

In conclusion: Ito follows or develops Lawrence's ideas, such as egocentrism and the utter loneliness of modern man, spontaneous life-flow and the balance of the mental and the physical (or intellectuality and sexuality) – which Ito must have thoroughly known from Lawrence's works. However, as *Transformations* shows, Ito follows traditional Japanese aesthetics instead of strict Christian morality in marriage – which is essential for Lawrence, as is evident in his essay 'A Propos of *Lady Chatterley's Lover*'. Ito discontinues the development of that sense of nature as vital life source, which is one of the most manifest and significant features throughout Lawrence's novels from *The White Peacock* (the earliest) to *Lady Chatterley's Lover* (the last).

Notes

1. As for Ito's translation of Lawrence's works, see *The Reception of D. H. Lawrence Around the World*, ed. Takeo Iida, pp. 233–5, 238–40.
2. Each of these novels was first published as a series in a monthly literary magazine in respective years. See *Shincho Nihon Bungaku Jiten* (*The Shincho Dictionary of Japanese Literature*), pp. 93–4.
3. My translation: all the subsequent quotations from Ito's works are my translations.
4. There would be, if any, one exception in Lawrence's novels: that is, Jack Grant in *The Boy in the Bush*. However, Jack cannot be equal to Ito's hero, Tatsuta. Because the novel ends just with a hint that Jack, who, being married to Monica, still needs another woman after he was refused by Mary (and then, giving up Mary, tells Hilda that he is willing to welcome her as his woman – while Hilda, too, would like to come back to and join him after Christmas). Since the reader is never told about what might happen afterwards to Jack, Monica and Hilda, we cannot equate their triangle relationship with that of Tastuta, Senko and Sakiko in Ito's *Transformations*. Still, Jack's claim of the urge of spontaneous sexuality towards two women – though he never takes any action to satisfy himself sexually with them both, as he wishes to – will be considered to be a challenge to the Christian moral code of monogamy: there is no other Lawrence novel, however, of such claim (except this Australian novel). Although Jack's claim of spontaneous sexuality is a little near to Tatsuta's, Ito is much more advanced and unique in creating Tatsuta in *Transformations* than is Lawrence in creating Jack in *The Boy in the Bush*.

CHAPTER 12

A RESPONSE TO KEITH CUSHMAN'S ' LAWRENCE'S DUST-JACKETS: ADDENDA AND CORRIGENDUM '

i

When I first read Keith Cushman's article 'Lawrence's Dust-Jackets: A Selection with Commentary' in *DHLR* 28 (1–2) (1999), his analysis of the colour dust jacket of *Tortoises* seemed accurate. However, after reading his 'Addenda and Corrigendum' in *DHLR* 29 (3) (2000), I started to question his conclusions and began to compare both the original Hiroshige turtle print and the Seltzer-published Lawrence dust jacket.

As it turns out, James T. Boulton and Lindeth Vasey's note on the dust jacket in *The Letters of D. H. Lawrence,* Volume v is inaccurate, although Cushman in his 2000 note claims that they 'have it right' (71). Boulton and Vasey's footnote glosses Lawrence's 20 November 1924 letter: 'It is a complete print, *Mannen Bridge* (*Fukagaka Mannen Bashi*), no. 51 of *100 Views of Edo* (*Meisho Edo Hyakkei*) (Tokyo, c. 1856–9)[1] by Ando Hiroshige (1797–1858): in the foreground, a turtle, for sale, is suspended in a window with Mt. Fuji seen across the river' (*L* v 175). However, my research shows that it is not 'a complete print', and their placement of the turtle within a 'window' seems erroneous.

Warren Roberts and Paul Poplawski's explanation of the same print is also misleading. They say that the

> upper cover (of *Tortoises*) is illustrated with a colour print by Hiroshige showing Mt. Fujiyama in the background and, in the foreground, a turtle is suspended from a scaffolding by a rope secured around his middle; at the bottom of the scaffolding in pseudo-oriental lettering (is written): TORTOISES (*double rule marking the base of the scaffolding*). (72)

Roberts posited this 'scaffolding' interpretation in both the 1963 first edition (53) and 1982 second edition (54) of *A Bibliography of D. H. Lawrence*. Poplawski's third edition presents the assertion unchanged. As we shall see the illustration's sophisticated framing presents neither a scaffold nor a window but an authentic, if unusual, perspective of 19th-century Japanese life.

A comparison of Hiroshige's *Fukagawa Mannen Bridge* (see Figure 1, reproduced from the portfolio *Meisho Edo Hyakkei* I) (in *Ukiyoe Taikei* (*Ukiyoe Series*), Shuei-sha Press) with the Seltzer dust jacket (see Figure 2)[2] reveals five discrepancies. First, in the far left of Hiroshige's original there is a raft with a man standing on it. The man is obscured on the dust jacket: only his staff is depicted. Second, in the bottom right corner of the original a man wears a round hat. However, on the dust jacket the hat has a more triangular shape.

There are differences in colour between the two turtle prints. First, the sunsets of the two illustrations differ. In the original, a white patch of sunlight cuts the top line of the reddening cloud on the left side of Mt. Fuji. However, on the dust jacket the white sunlight is dominated by a reddening cloud on the left side of Mt. Fuji. Next, the upper sky and the sides of the river are blue in the original, while on the dust jacket they are pale green. Lastly, different colours are used on both illustrations' 'frame' (or 'scaffolding', to use Roberts's terminology). The dust jacket presents a mid-ground frame in light yellow or brown corresponding to the yellow or brown of the foreground frame. In the original, the mid-ground frame is dark or blackish brown and the foreground frame is pale yellow.

Aside from these differences, the four Japanese names in Hiroshige's original print are erased on the dust jacket. In the top right corner there is the title of the series: *Meisho Edo Hyakkei* (*100 Views of Edo*). To the left of it is the title of this print: *Fukagawa Mannen Bashi* (*Fukagawa Mannen Bridge*). In the bottom left there is 'Hiroshige Ga', which means that it was painted by Hiroshige. In the bottom left corner there is the abbreviated name of the print producer 'Uoei'. (His full name is Uoya Eikichi.) All these names are cleanly erased from Lawrence's dust jacket. (On the uppermost top right margin of Hiroshige's print there are two Chinese characters encircled: they are probably seals, though I am not sure what they are there for and whose they are. They have been eliminated from the dust jacket as well).

Noticing these differences between Seltzer's dust jacket and Hiroshige's print we can conclude that the dust jacket itself is not 'a complete print' or 'a colour print' by Hiroshige (as Lawrence, Boulton and Vasey believe or as Roberts and Poplawski assert). The whole picture is most likely a copy by an unknown illustrator talented enough to deceive Lawrence and the editors of both the CUP *Letters* and *A Bibliography of D.H. Lawrence*. As Cushman notes in his 1999 article, 'what we're actually looking at is a *later* Japanese print which incorporates Hiroshige's print' (42). If by 'a *later* Japanese print' Cushman means a professional copy, then he is no doubt accurate. But whether that '*later* Japanese print' is truly a Japanese one is hard to determine. A professional illustrator and copyist would be able to imitate Hiroshige's print fairly accurately, whether he or she is Japanese, English, or even American.

I must mention the illustrations' complex visual framing, where our view of both the turtle and of Mt. Fuji is bordered by what appear to be (particularly to western viewers) a complicated wooden 'scaffolding' (Boulton and Vasey) or multiple 'window' frames (Roberts and Poplawksi). In reality the foregrounds of both the painting and the dust jacket are dominated by the presence of a round, wooden tub. The brown or yellow curved 'double rule(d)' lines at the bottom of the dust jacket parallel the more clearly-represented encircling boards of the tub in the original: neither are 'the base of the scaffolding' at all. The turtle is suspended by thin ropes not from any 'scaffolding' but from the handle of the tub or bucket – which is depicted in the top left – extending out of view at the picture's right-hand corner. The mid-ground frame is neither a windowsill nor a scaffold but the bottom of the railing along the wooden Fukagawa Mannen Bridge.

To further understand the illustration's perspective it is helpful to have a more complete view of Fukagawa Mannen Bridge from a different angle: *Below Fukagawa Mannen Bridge* (*Fukagawa Mannen Bashi Shita*) painted by another outstanding Japanese painter, Katsushika Hokusai (1760–1849), Hiroshige's contemporary and one of his greatest rivals (see Figure 3) (in *Ukiyoe Taikei*, Shueisha Press). It is the fourth in Hokusai's famous series: *36 Views of Mount Fuji* (*Fugoku Sanjuu Rokkei*) and it shows the entire bridge, with Mt. Fuji seen across the river in the background. In clear view are the many oblong openings of the railing, which consists of 28 vertical bars and two curving bars running from end to end (one at the top of the railing and one at its middle). Placing, next to the railing, a tub with a handle from which a turtle is suspended by a rope will provide a similar composition to that created by Hiroshige in the turtle print. The complicated visual design can easily mislead viewers: a greater understanding of the cultural context leads to a broader understanding of both illustrations: print and book jacket.

Cushman, in his 1999 article, also claims that 'the suspended turtle (not tortoise) is looking at Mt. Fujiyama' (71). At first glance the turtle does seem to be looking at Mount Fuji across the river. Perhaps it may be looking at Japan's most beautiful mountain while suspended in the air but it is more likely that the turtle, suspended from the handle of a street peddler's wooden bucket, is waiting to be bought and thrown into the river below. Shigewo Miyao, a Ukiyoe expert, comments on Hiroshige's *Fukagawa Mannen Bashi*:

> It is said that in Hiroshige's time street pedlars used to sell turtles (or carps or eels) to pedestrians on bridges or along riversides or on streets in order to make money by trying to urge the pedestrians to perform for the animals the merciful act of buying and throwing one or some of the animals into the river. This was because Buddhism taught that saving animals was a merciful act and it promised salvation to the mercy-givers after their death, though it is not certain whether the benefactors would surely be sent to heaven. Although there is no record left that such animals as turtles, carps or eels were actually sold on Fukagawa Mannen Bridge it seems to me that Hiroshige incorporated the motif of such a daily pedlar's habit into this print composition and painted the pedlar's suspended turtle. (*Meisho Edo Hyakkei* I 115) (my translation)

19th-century street pedlars carried the turtles or carps or eels in a wooden tub for sale. (Even during my childhood such pedlars carrying wooden buckets full of live fish could be found: nowadays they have been replaced by supermarkets). In Hiroshige's print the wooden tub of an unseen street pedlar is placed on the bridge and the turtle is suspended by a cord from its handle for sale: the turtle waits for his or her own agent of potential salvation.

There is another theory, according to Miyao, as to why the turtle is depicted in association with Mannen Bridge. Mannen means ten thousand years in Japanese (and Fukagawa is, in passing, a place name). One Japanese proverb says that 'Tsuru wa Sennen, Kame wa Mannen' (which means that cranes live for one thousand years and turtles for ten thousand years). Both are Japanese symbols of longevity. So the turtle (symbolizing ten-thousand-year longevity), Miyao adds, echoes the name of Mannen (ten thousand years) Bridge *(Meisho Edo Hyakkei* I 115).

'I understood it (the colour print) was a complete print, yet the view is surely Hiroshige's', wrote Lawrence in his 20 November 1924 letter (*L* v 175). From the date of that letter up to Roberts and Poplawski's 2001 CUP *Bibliography*, Lawrence's original understanding of Hiroshige's so-called 'complete print' has been generally accepted as fact. Let us now accept that the colour dust jacket is not 'a complete print' but an imitation of Hiroshige's.[3] It is probable that what Lawrence actually saw was a copy, not Hiroshige's original: nor did he ever compare the two prints. If he had, Lawrence's sharp painter's eye may have noticed the differences listed above. Evidently, the dust jacket that Lawrence saw was an unknown artist's excellent copy of Hiroshige's *Fukagawa Mannen Bridge*.

Boulton and Vasey's note and Roberts and Poplawski's explanation will need revision in their future editions so that readers of Lawrence can understand the true composition of the turtle dust jacket and its original Hiroshige print. I also hope that Hiroshige's intent of the internationally known *Fukagawa Mannen Bridge* will not be distorted by the inaccurate notes of these distinguished Lawrentians.

In his 1999 article Cushman asks: 'what if Lawrence wrote his tortoise poems in Italy and they have nothing to do with Japan?'(42). However, if the turtle in the dust jacket is imploring passers-by – or the painter himself – for help or mercy then its cry may, I think, have something to do with Lawrence's poetic tortoise shout. Therefore the dust jacket is not necessarily unconnected with the tortoise poems. At any rate Lawrence's dust jacket turtle and Hiroshige's, too – seeing the river below – seem to want to plunge quickly into it and feel at home in the shadow of Mt. Fuji.

Notes

1. Boulton and Vasey note that *Meisho Edo Hyakkei* was published in 'c. 1856–9'. In fact it was published from 1856 until his death in 1858 (see *Nippon Dai Hyakka Zensho* vol. 3, p. 132).

2. The colour print of Hiroshige's *Fukagawa Mannen Bridge* and Lawrence's colour dust jacket of *Tortoises* are also available on the websites (http://hiroshige100.blog91.fc2.com/blog-entry-52.html) and (http://www.gutenberg.org/files/22475/22475-h/22475-h.htm).

3. One of the imitations of Hiroshige's *Fukagawa Mannen Bridge* which Lawrence might have seen is Champfleury's 1870 dust jacket for his edition of *L'Imagerie Nouvelle* (Figure 4, *Japonisme* 57). Hiroshige's paintings had been so popular in the west after the Paris world exhibition of 1867 (where lots of Japanese works of art, including some by Ukiyoe were displayed) and Japonism made a great impact on western artists. After that event, according to Genevieve Lacambre, 'Hiroshige's Ukiyoe paintings would have been introduced into Paris in book form and must have been easily available' (Lacambre 21: my translation). Therefore, Champfleury could easily have used Hiroshige's print for his dust jacket. A comparison of Hiroshige's print with Champfleury's dust jacket also reveals that the latter is almost an exact imitation of the former. It seems that Champfleury's dust jacket might have been used or consulted for Lawrence's 1921 tortoise one.

'Figure 1: *Fukagawa Mannen Bridge*'

'Figure 2: D H Lawrence *Tortoises*'

4 深川万年橋下 大判錦絵

'Figure 3: *Below Fukagawa Mannen Bridge*'

'Figure 4: *L'Imagerie Nouvelle*'

BIBLIOGRAPHY

1.   Works by D. H. Lawrence

Amores. London: Duckworth, 1916.

Apocalypse and the Writings on Revelation, ed. Mara Kalnins. Cambridge: Cambridge University Press, 1980.

'A Propos of *Lady Chatterley's Lover*'. *Lady Chatterley's Lover. A Propos of Lady Chatterley's Lover*, ed. Michael Squires. Cambridge: Cambridge University Press, 1993. 305–35.

'Aristocracy'. *Reflections on the Death of a Porcupine and Other Essays,* ed. Michael Herbert. Cambridge: Cambridge University Press, 1988. 367–76.

The Boy in the Bush (with M. L. Skinner), ed. Paul Eggert. Cambridge: Cambridge University Press, 1990.

The Complete Poems of D. H. Lawrence, ed. Vivian de Sola Pinto and Warren Roberts. Harmondsworth: Penguin, 1977.

'David'. *The Plays,* ed. Hans-Wilhelm Schwarze and John Worthen. Cambridge: Cambridge University Press, 1999. 433–525.

'Education of the People'. *Reflections on the Death of a Porcupine and Other Essays,* ed. Michael Herbert. Cambridge: Cambridge University Press, 1988. 85–166.

'The Escaped Cock'. *The Virgin and the Gipsy and Other Stories,* ed. Michael Herbert, Bethan Jones and Lindeth Vasey. Cambridge: Cambridge University Press, 2005. 123–63.

'Fantasia of the Unconscious'. *Psychoanalysis and the Unconscious and Fantasia of the Unconscious,* ed. Bruce Steele. Cambridge: Cambridge University Press, 2004. 44–204.

The First and Second Lady Chatterley Novels, ed. Dieter Mehl and Christa Jansohn. Cambridge: Cambridge University Press. 1999.

The Fox, The Captain's Doll, The Ladybird, ed. Dieter Mehl. Cambridge: Cambridge University Press, 1992.

'The Fox'. *The Fox, The Captain's Doll, The Ladybird,* ed. Dieter Mehl. Cambridge: Cambridge University Press, 1992. 7–71.

'The Georgian Renaissance: Review of *Georgian Poetry:1911–12'. Introductions and Reviews,* ed. N. H. Reeve and John Worthen. Cambridge: Cambridge University Press, 2005. 199–204.

'Hymns in a Man's Life'. *Late Essays and Articles,* ed. James T. Boulton. Cambridge: Cambridge University Press. 2004. 130–34.

Introductions and Reviews, ed. N. H. Reeve and John Worthen. Cambridge: Cambridge University Press, 2005.

'Introduction to These Paintings'. *Late Essays and Articles,* ed. James T.Boulton. Cambridge: Cambridge University Press, 2004. 182–217.

Kangaroo, ed. Bruce Steele. Cambridge: Cambridge University Press, 1994.

Lady Chatterley's Lover. A Propos of 'Lady Chatterley's Lover', ed. Michael Squires. Cambridge: Cambridge University Press, 1993.

'The Ladybird'. *The Fox, The Captain's Doll, The Ladybird,* ed. Dieter Mehl. Cambridge: Cambridge University Press, 1992. 155–221.

'The Last Laugh'. *The Woman Who Rode Away and Other Stories,* ed. Dieter Mehl and Christa Jansohn. Cambridge: Cambridge University Press, 1995. 122–37.

Last Poems, ed. Richard Aldington and Giuseppe Orioli. Florence: Orioli, 1932; London: Martin Secker, 1933.

Late Essays and Articles, ed. James T. Boulton. Cambridge: Cambridge University Press, 2004.

The Letters of D. H. Lawrence. Vol. I: 1901–13, ed. James T. Boulton. Cambridge: Cambridge University Press, 1979.

The Letters of D. H. Lawrence. Vol. II: 1913–16, ed. George J. Zytaruk and James T. Boulton. Cambridge: Cambridge University Press, 1981.

The Letters of D. H. Lawrence. Vol. III: October 1916–June 1921, ed. James T. Boulton and Andrew Robertson. Cambridge: Cambridge University Press, 1984.

The Letters of D. H. Lawrence. Vol. IV: 1921–24, ed. Warren Robert, James T. Boulton and Elizabeth Mansfield. Cambridge: Cambridge University Press, 1987.

The Letters of D. H. Lawrence. Vol. V: 1924–27, ed. James T Boulton & Lindeth Vasey. Cambridge: Cambridge University Press, 1989.

Love Poems and Others. London: Duckworth, 1913.

'Making Pictures' . *Late Essays and Articles,* ed. James T. Boulton. Cambridge: Cambridge University Press, 2004. 225–35.

'Mornings in Mexico'. *Mornings in Mexico and Other Essays,* ed. Virginia Crosswhite Hyde. Cambridge: Cambridge University Press, 2009. 7–99.

Mornings in Mexico and Other Essays, ed. Virginia Crosswhite Hyde. Cambridge: Cambridge University Press, 2009.

'New Mexico'. *Mornings in Mexico and Other Essays,* ed. Virginia Crosswhite Hyde. Cambridge: Cambridge University Press, 2009. 173–81.

'On Being Religious'. *Reflections on the Death of a Porcupine and Other Essays,* ed. Michael Herbert. Cambridge: Cambridge University Press, 1988. 187–93.

'The Overtone'. *St Mawr and Other Stories,* ed. Brian Finney. Cambridge: Cambridge University Press, 1983. 3–17.

'Pan in America'. *Mornings in Mexico and Other Essays,* ed. Virginia Crosswhite Hyde. Cambridge: Cambridge University Press, 2009. 153–64.

Pansies. London: Martin Secker, 1929.

The Plays, ed. Hans-Wilhelm Schwarze and John Worthen. Cambridge: Cambridge University Press, 1999. 433–525.

The Plumed Serpent, ed. L. D. Clark. Cambridge: Cambridge University Press, 1987.

The Poems of D. H. Lawrence. 2 vols., ed. Christopher Pollnitz. Cambridge: Cambridge University Press, 2013.

Psychoanalysis and the Unconscious and Fantasia of the Unconscious, ed. Bruce Steele. Cambridge: Cambridge University Press, 2004.

The Rainbow, ed. Mark Kinkead-Weekes. Cambridge: Cambridge University Press, 1989.

'The Reality of Peace'. *Reflections on the Death of a Porcupine and Other Essays,* ed. Michael Herbert. Cambridge: Cambridge University Press, 1988. 25–52.

Reflections on the Death of a Porcupine and Other Essays, ed. Michael
    Herbert. Cambridge: Cambridge University Press, 1988.

Sketches of Etruscan Places and Other Italian Essays, ed. Simonetta de
    Philippis. Cambridge: Cambridge University Press, 1992.

Sons and Lovers, ed. Carl and Helen Baron. Cambridge: Cambridge
    University Press, 1992.

'St. Mawr'. *St. Mawr and Other Stories*, ed. Brian Finney. Cambridge:
    Cambridge University Press, 1983.19–155.

St. Mawr and Other Stories, ed. Brian Finney. Cambridge: Cambridge
    University Press, 1983.

Studies in Classic American Literature, ed. Ezra Greenspan, Lindeth
    Vasey and John Worthen. Cambridge: Cambridge University Press,
    2003.

'Study of Thomas Hardy'. *Study of Thomas Hardy and Other Essays,* ed.
    Bruce Steele. Cambridge: Cambridge University Press, 1985. 3–128.

'Sun'. *The Woman Who Rode Away and Other Stories,* ed. Dieter Mehl
    and Christa Jansohn. Cambridge: Cambridge University Press,
    1995. 19–38.

Tortoises. New York: Thomas Seltzer, 1921.

Tortoises. http://www.gutenberg.org/files/22475/22475-h/22475-h.htm
    (28 December, 2013) (electronic version of the above 1921 Seltzer
    edition)

'Twilight in Italy'. *Twilight in Italy and Other Essays,* ed. Paul Eggert.
    Cambridge: Cambridge University Press, 1994. 85–226.

The Virgin and the Gipsy and Other Stories, ed. Michael Herbert, Bethan
    Jones and Lindeth Vasey. Cambridge: Cambridge University Press,
    2005.

The White Peacock, ed. Andrew Robertson. Cambridge: Cambridge
    University Press, 1983.

'The Woman Who Rode Away'. *The Woman Who Rode Away and
    Other Stories,* ed. Dieter Mehl and Christa Jansohn. Cambridge:
    Cambridge University Press, 1995. 39–71.

The Woman Who Rode Away and Other Stories, ed. Dieter Mehl and
    Christa Jansohn. Cambridge: Cambridge University Press, 1995.

Women in Love, ed. David Farmer, Lindeth Vasey and John Worthen.
    Cambridge: Cambridge University Press, 1987.

2. Other Works Cited

Anderson, William. *Green Man: the Archetype of our Oneness with the Earth.* Photography by Clive Hicks. Fakenham, England: Compassbooks, 1998.

Apuleius, Lucius. *The Golden Ass*, trans. Robert Graves. Harmondsworth: Penguin, 1972.

Asahi, Chiseki. 'D. H. Lawrence to Ito Sei'('D. H. Lawrence and Sei Ito'). *Kokubungaku: Kaishaku to Kanshou* (*Japanese Literature: Interpretations and Appreciations*), 60 (11) (1995). 45–51.

Barker, Anne Darlington. 'Fairy Tale and St. Mawr'. *Forum for Modern Language Studies* 20 (1) (1984). 76–83.

Barrett, George S., ed. *Congregational Church Hymnal.* London: Congregational Union of England and Wales, 1877.

Beichman, Janine. *Embracing the Firebird: Yosano Akiko and the Birth of the Female Voice in Modern Japanese Poetry.* Hawaii: University of Hawaii Press, 2002.

Bell, Michael, Keith Cushman, Takeo Iida and Hiro Tateishi, eds. *D. H. Lawrence: Literature, History, Culture.* Tokyo: Kokusho Kankoukai Press, 2005.

Björkén, Cecilia. *Into the Isle of Self: Nietzschean Patterns and Contrasts in D. H. Lawrence's* The Trespasser. Lund Studies in English 89. Lund: Lund University Press, 1996.

Blavatsky, H. P. *The Secret Doctrine.* Vol. I. California: Theosophical University Press, 1977.

Boulton, James T. 'Introduction'. *The Letters of D. H. Lawrence.* Vol. I. Cambridge: Cambridge University Press, 1979. 1–20.

Brewster, Earl and Achsah. *D. H. Lawrence: Reminiscences and Correspondence.* London: Martin Secker, 1934.

Bungakukai (*The World of Literature*). No. 40 (1896) ('Lady Godiva'); No. 42 (1896) ('Love Dream'); No. 43. (1896) (Titian's 'Sleeping Venus'); No. 58 (1898) ('A Waiting Maid of Diana').

Burnet, John. *Early Greek Philosophy* 1892. 4th ed. London: Adam and Charles Black, 1930.

Burwell, Rose Marie. 'A Catalogue of D. H. Lawrence's Reading from Early Childhood'. *The D. H. Lawrence Review* 3 (Autumn 1970). 193–324.

Campbell, Roy, trans. *The Poems of St. John of the Cross.* The Spanish text with a translation with a preface by Martin C. D'Arcy, S. J. London: The Harvill Press, 1952.

Carter, Frederic. *D. H. Lawrence and the Body Mystical.* London: Denis Archer, 1932.

Cavitch, David. *D. H. Lawrence and the New World.* New York: Oxford University Press, 1969.

Cipolla, Elizabeth. 'The Last Poems of D. H. Lawrence'. *The D. H. Lawrence Review* 2 (Summer 1969). 103–19.

Clark, L. D. *Dark Night of the Body: D. H. Lawrence's* The Plumed Serpent. Austin: University of Texas Press, 1964.

The Cloud of Unknowing, trans. into modern English with an introduction by Clifton Wolters. Harmondsworth: Penguin, 1977.

Congregational Church Hymnal, ed. George S. Barrett. London: Congregational Union of England and Wales, 1877.

Cowan, James C. 'Allusions and Symbols in D. H. Lawrence's *The Escaped Cock'. Critical Essays on D. H. Lawrence,* ed. Dennis Jackson and Fleda Brown Jackson. Boston: GK Hall, 1988. 174–88.

Cowan, James C. *D. H. Lawrence's American Journey: A Study in Literature and Myth*. Cleveland: The Press of Case Western Reserve University, 1970.

Crossley-Holland, Kevin, ed. *Folk-Tales in the British Isles*. London: Faber & Faber, 1985.

Cushman, Keith. 'Lawrence's Dust-Jackets: A Selection with Commentary'. *DHLR* 28 (1–2) (1999). 29–52.

Cushman, Keith. 'Lawrentiana: Lawrence's Dust-Jackets: Addenda and Corrigendum'. *DHLR* 29 (3) (2000). 71–2.

de Filippis, Simonetta and Nick Ceramella, eds . *D. H. Lawrence and Literary Genre*. Napoli: Loffredo Editore, 2004.

de Sola Pinto, Vivian. 'Introduction'. *The Complete Poems of D. H. Lawrence,* ed. Vivian de Sola Pinto and Warren Roberts. Harmondsworth: Penguin, 1977. 1–21.

Dionysius the Areopagite. *The Divine Names and the Mystical Theology,* trans. C. E. Rolt. London: SPCK, 1979.

Durr, Robert A. *Poetic Vision and the Psychedelic Experience*. New York: Syracuse University Press, 1970.

E.T. (Chambers, Jessie). *D. H. Lawrence: A Personal Record*. 2nd ed. London: Cass, 1965.

Ellis, David. *D. H Lawrence: Dying Game. 1922–1930*. Cambridge: Cambridge University Press, 1998.

Frazer, James G. *The Golden Bough: A Study in Magic and Religion*. Abridged edition. London: Macmillan, 1922.

Fry, Rosalie K. *Child of the Western Isles*. London: JM Dent and Sons, 1957.

Fry, Rosalie K. *Whistler in the Mist*. New York: Farrar, Straus and Giroux, 1968.

Frye, Northrop, ed. *Paradise Lost and Selected Poetry and Prose*. New York: Rinehart, 1957.

Fukuzwa, Yukichi. 'Danjo Kosai Ron' ('On the Intercourse between Man and Woman'). *Fukuzawa Yukichi Zenshu* (*The Collected Works of Yukichi Fukuzawa*). Vol. 5. Tokyo: Iwanami-shoten, 1970. 583–605.

Gajdusek, Robert E. 'A Reading of *The White Peacock*'. *A D. H. Lawrence Miscellany,* ed. Harry T. Moore. London: Heinemann, 1961. 188–203.

Gilbert, Sandra M. *Acts of Attention: The Poems of D. H. Lawrence*. Ithaca and London: Cornell University Press, 1972.

Goldstein, Sanford and Seishi Shinoda. 'Notes'. *Tangled Hair: Selected Tanka from 'Midaregami',* trans. Sanford Goldstein and Seishi Shinoda. Tokyo: Charles E. Tuttle, 1987. 123–65.

Griffiths, Bede. *Return to the Centre*. London: Collins, 1976.

Gutierrez, Donald. 'D. H. Lawrence's 'Spirit of Place' as Eco-Monism'. *The Journal of the D. H. Lawrence Society 1991*. 39–50.

Haga, Toru. *Midaregami no Keifu: Shi to E no Hikakubungaku* (*The Genealogy of Tangled Hair: Comparative Literature of Poetry and Paintings*). Tokyo: Bijutsukoron-sha Press, 1981.

Hagen, Patricia. *Metaphor's Way of Knowing: The Poetry of D. H. Lawrence and the Church of Mechanism*. New York: Peter Lang, 1995.

Heine, Heinrich. *Zur Geschichte der Religion und Philosophie in Deutchland*, trans. Yoshifumi Mori, *Heine Sanbun Sakuhinshu* (*Heine's Prose Works*). Vol. 4. Kyoto: Shorai-sha Press, 1994.

Heine, Heinrich. 'Die Göttin Diana', trans. Yoko Nagura, *Doitsu Romanha Zenshu* (*The Collected Works of German Romantics*). Vol. 16. Tokyo: Kokusho Kankoukai Press, 1989.

Heywood, Christopher. '*Birds, Beasts and Flowers*: the Evolutionary Context and an African Literary Source'. *Rethinking Lawrence,* ed. Keith Brown. Milton Keynes: Open University Press, 1990. 151–62.

Hirano, Ken. 'Ito Sei'. *Kindai Bugaku Daijiten* (*The Grand Dictionary of Modem Japanese Literature*). Vol. I., ed. Kindaibungakukan. Tokyo: Kodan-sha Press, 1977. 141–4.

Hiratsuka, Raicho. 'Boseihogo no Shucho wa Iraishuginiarazu'. ('State-protected Motherhood is Not the Insistence on State-Dependency'). *Hiratsuka Raicho Chosakushu* (*Selected Works of Raicho Hiratsuka*). Vol. 2. Tokyo: Ootsuki Shoten, 1983. 350–9.

Hiratsuka, Raicho. *Hiratsuka Raicho Chosakushu* (*Selected Works of Raicho Hiratsuka*). Vols. 2 and 3. Tokyo: Ootsuki Shoten, 1983.

Hiroshige. "Fukagawa Mannen Bridge". (Meisho Edo Hyakkei). http://hiroshige100.blog91.fc2.com/blog-entry-52.html (28 December, 2013)

The Holy Bible. London and New York: Collin's Clear-Type Press, no date.

Hough, Graham. *The Dark Sun: A Study of D. H. Lawrence*. London: Gerald Duckworth, 1968.

Humma, John B. 'Of Bits, Beasts and Bush: The Interior Wilderness in D. H. Lawrence's *Kangaroo*'. *South Atlantic Review* 50 (1), 1986. Reprinted in *D. H. Lawrence: Critical Assessments*. Vol. II, ed. David Ellis and Ornella De Zordo. Mountfield: Helm Information, Inc., 1992. 506–20.

Hutchinson, F. E., ed. *The Works of George Herbert*, with a commentary by F. E. Hutchinson. Oxford: Oxford University Press, 1978.

Ichikawa, Shuji. 'Thomas Traherne and Dionysius the Areopagite'. *Studies in English Literature* (Tokyo: Literary Society of Japan) 48 (1972). 199–215.

Iida, Takeo. 'A Response to Keith Cushman's "Lawrence's Dust-Jackets: Addenda and Corrigendum"'. *DHLR* 31 (3) (2003). 43–7.

Iida, Takeo. 'D. H. Lawrence and Akiko Yosano: Contemporary Poets of Human Touch and Cosmic Life'. *D. H. Lawrence: Literature,*

History, Culture, ed. Keith Cushman, Michael Bell, Takeo Iida and Hiro Tateishi. Tokyo: Kokusho Kankoukai Press, 2005. 111–31.

Iida, Takeo. 'D. H. Lawrence and Sei Ito: Characteristics of the Sexual Scenes in Their Novels'. *Comparative Cultural Studies of Kurume University*. 25 (2000). 137–49.

Iida, Takeo. 'D. H. Lawrence: the Bible and the Mystics'. *Etudes Lawrenciennes* 35 (2007). 87–99.

Iida, Takeo. 'D. H. Lawrence's "The Ship of Death" and Other Poems in *Last Poems'. Studies in English Literature* (Tokyo: Literary Society of Japan) 58 (1) (1981). 33–47.

Iida, Takeo. 'Lawrence's Pagan Gods and Christianity'. *The D. H. Lawrence Review* 23 (12–13) (1991). 179–90.

Iida, Takeo. 'Lawrence's Pan Worship and Green Man Image'. *D. H. Lawrence Studies* (Korea). 12 (3) (2004). 233–47.

Iida, Takeo. 'Nature Deities: Reawakening Blood Consciousness in the Europeans'. *Etudes Lawrenciennes* 10 (1994). 27–42.

Iida, Takeo. 'On a Topos Called the Sun Shining at Midnight in D. H. Lawrence's Poetry'. *The D. H. Lawrence Review* 15 (3) (1982). 271–90.

Iida, Takeo, ed. *The Reception of D. H. Lawrence Around the World*. Fukuoka: Kyushu University Press, 1999.

Iida, Takeo. '*St. Mawr, The Escaped Cock* and *Child of the Western Isles*: the Revival of an Animistic Worldview in the Modern World'. *The Journal of the D. H. Lawrence Society 1999* (UK). 23–35.

Iida, Takeo. 'The Universality of D. H. Lawrence's Animistic Vision'. *D. H. Lawrence and Literary Genre,* ed. Simonetta de Filippis and Nick Ceramella. Napoli: Loffredo Editore, 2004. 257–66.

Iida, Takeo. 'The World of Animism in Contrast with Christianity in *St. Mawr'. The Journal of the D. H. Lawrence Society 1997*. 32–46.

Immoos, Thomas. 'Die Sonne leuchtet um Mitternacht: ein literarischer und religionsgeschichtlicher Topos in Ost und West'. *Analytische Psychologie* (Karger, Basel) 6 (1977), 482–500; trans. into Japanese by K. Ozaki, in *Sophia* (Sophia University, Tokyo) 24 (1) (1975). 22–40.

Imura, Kimie. *Keruto no Shinwa* (*Celtic Mythology*). Tokyo: Chikuma Shobou, 1983.

Inge, William Rauf. *Christian Mysticism*. 1899. 5th ed. London: Methuen, 1921.

Ito, Sei. 'Chatterley Fujin no Koibito no Seibyosha no Tokushitsu'. ('Characteristics of the Sexual Scenes in *Lady Chatterley's Lover*'). *Ito Sei Zenshu* (*The Collected Works of Sei Ito*). Vol. 16. Tokyo: Shincho-sha Press, 1972. 640–55.

Ito, Sei. *Excavations. Ito Sei Zenshu* (*The Collected Works of Sei Ito*). Vol. 10. Tokyo: Shincho-sha Press, 1972. 5–350.

Ito, Sei. *Josei ni Kansuru Junishou* (*Twelve Chapters Concerning Women*). Tokyo: Kadokawa-shoten, 1960.

Ito, Sei. *Transformations. Ito Sei Zenshu* (*The Collected Works of Sei Ito*). Vol. 10. Tokyo: Shincho-sha Press, 1972. 351–593.

Izutsu, Toshihiko. *Shinpi Tetsugaku dai nibu: Shinpishugi no Girisha Tetsugakuteki Tenkai* (*Mystic Philosophy Part II: Greek Philosophical Developments of Mysticism*). Kyoto: Jinbiuishoin, 1978.

Jackson, Dennis. 'The 'Old Pagan Vision': Myth and Ritual in *Lady Chatterley's Lover*'. *The D. H. Lawrence Review* 11(3) (1978): 260–71; expanded in *Critical Essays on D. H. Lawrence*, ed. Dennis Jackson and Fleda Brown Jackson. Boston: GK Hall, 1988. 128–44.

Jarrett-Kerr, Martin, C.R. (Father William Tiverton). *D. H. Lawrence and Human Existence*. New York: Chip's Bookshop, 1971.

Johnston, William *The Mysticism of the Cloud of Unknowing* with a foreword by Thomas Merton. Wheathampstead: Anthony Clarke, 1978.

Jones, Bethan. *The Last Poems of D. H. Lawrence: Shaping a Late Style*. Farnham: Ashgate, 2010.

Jung, C. G. *On the Psychology of the Unconscious* in *Two Essays on Analytical Psychology,* trans. R. F. C. Hull. Princeton, New Jersey: Princeton University Press, 1977.

Jung, C. G. *Psychology and Alchemy,* trans. R. F. C. Hull. Princeton, New Jersey: Princeton University Press, 1977.

Kalnins, Mara. 'Introduction'. *Apocalypse and the Writings on Revelation.* Cambridge: Cambridge University Press, 1980. 3–38.

Kitamura, Tokoku. 'Shojo no Junketsu wo Ronzu'. ('On the Chastity of a Virgin'). *Kitamura Tokoku Senshu (Selected Works of Tokoku Kitamura)*, ed. Katsumoto Seiichiro. Iwanami Library. Tokyo: Iwanami-shoten, 1960. 187–95.

Knight, George W. *Neglected Powers:Essays on 19th and 20th century Literature*. London: Routledge and Kegan Paul, 1971.

Kobayashi, Tadashi. ed. *Fugoku Sanjuu Rokkei (36 Views of Mt. Fuji by Katsushika Hokusai)*. *Ukiyoe Taikei (Ukiyoe Series)*. Vol. 13. Tokyo: Shuei-sha Press: 1976.

Kobayashi, Tomie. 'Kaisetsu' ('Introduction'). *Hiratsuka Raicho Chosakushu (Selected Works of Raicho Hiratsuka)*. Vol. 3. Tokyo: Ootsuki Shoten, 1983. 367–82.

Kojiki: Ancient Record of Japan, trans. Donald Philippi. Tokyo: University of Tokyo Press, 1968.

Kokuritsu Seiyo Bijutsukan Gakugeika (Fine Arts Division of National Museum of Western Arts), ed. *Japonism*. Tokyo: Kokuritsu Seiyo Bijutsukan (National Museum of Western Arts), 1988.

Kouno, Tetsuji. *D. H. Lawrence no Kaiga to Bungaku (Paintings and Works of D. H. Lawrence)*. Osaka: Sogen-sha Press, 2000.

Lacambre, Genevieve. 'Jukyuseiki no Japonisumu no Kigen' ('The Origin of Japonism in the 19th Century'). *Japonism,* ed. Kokuritsu Seiyo Bijutsukan Gakugeika(Fine Arts Division of National Museum of Western Arts). Tokyo: Kokuritsu Seiyo Bijutsukan (National Museum of Western Arts), 1988. 17–24.

Law, William. *The Works of the Reverend William Law*. Vol. VII. London: Printed for M. Richardson, 1749.

LeDoux, Larry V. 'Christ and Isis: The Function of the Dying and Reviving God in *The Man Who Died*'. *The D. H. Lawrence Review* 5 (2) (1972). 132–48.

Lee, C. J. P. *The Metaphysics of Mass Art-Cultural Ontology*. Vol. 1: Mysticism, Mexico and English Literature. Lewiston: The Edwin Mellen Press, 1999.

Lindsay, Jack. 'The Impact of Modernism on Lawrence'. *Paintings of D. H. Lawrence,* ed. Mervin Levy. London: Cory, Adams & Mackay, 1964. 35–53.

Maloney, George A., S. J. *Inward Stillness.* New Jersey: Dimension Books, 1976.

Marshall, Tom. *The Psychic Mariner: A Reading of the Poems of D. H. Lawrence.* New York: The Viking Press, 1970.

Martin, L. C., ed. *Henry Vaughan: Poetry and Selected Prose.* Oxford: Oxford University Press, 1963.

Merivale, Patricia. *Pan the Goat-God: His Myth in Modern Times.* Cambridge, Massachusetts: Harvard University Press, 1969.

The Methodist Hymn Book, with Tunes. London: Wesleyan Conference Office, 1904.

Meyers, Jeffrey. *Katherine Mansfield: A Biography.* London: Hamish Hamilton, 1978.

Millett, Robert W. *The Vultures and the Phoenix: A Study of the Mandrake Press Edition of D. H. Lawrence's Paintings.* London and Toronto: Associated University Presses, 1983.

Miyao, Shigwo, ed. *Meisho Edo Hyakkei* (*100 Views of Edo* by Hiroshige). Parts 1 and 2. *Ukiyoe Taikei* (*Ukiyoe Series*). Vols. 16 and 17. Tokyo: Shuei-sha Press, 1976.

Moore, Harry T. 'D. H. Lawrence and his Paintings'. *Paintings of D. H. Lawrence,* ed. Mervin Levy. London: Cory, Adams & Mackay, 1964. 17–34.

Mori, Haruhide. 'Kitsune no Buntai (The Literary Style of *The Fox*)'. *D. H. Lawrence Kitsume to Tekusuto* (*Readings of The Fox*), ed. Takao Tomiyama and Hiromichi Tateishi (Tokyo: Kokusho Kankoukai Press, 1994. 182–206.

Mori, Ohgai. 'Tsukikusa'. *Ohgai Zenshu* (*The Collected Works of Ohgai*). Vol. 23. Tokyo: Iwanami-shoten, 1973. 294–301.

Morisaki, Kazue and Keiji Sunouchi. *Genseirin ni Kaze ga Fuku* (*The Wind Blows Through a Primitive Forest*). Tokyo: Iwanami-shoten, 1996.

Morisaki, Kazue. *Chikyu no Inori* (*The Prayer of the Earth*). Tokyo: Shinyasousho-sha Press, 1998.

Murray, Gilbert. *Five Stages of Greek Religion.* Oxford; Oxford University Press, 1925.

Myojo (*Morning Star*). No. 5 (1900), 9 (an anonymous painting of two women bathing in a lake); No. 8 (1900), 7 (Heizoy Karl August's 'Marmorschön'); No.10 (1901), 36 (an anonymous drawing of

'Venus de Milo'); No.11 (1901), 5 (Titian's 'Sleeping Venus'); No. 13 (1901), 16 (P. Horter's art nouveau design).

Nagura, Yoko. 'On Die Göttin Diana'. *Heine Kenkyu* (*Studies on Heine*) 8 (1993), 121–41.

Nahal, Chaman. *D. H. Lawrence: An Eastern View.* South Brunswick and New York: A. S. Barnes and Co., 1970.

Nehls, Edward, ed. *D. H. Lawrence: A Composite Biography.* Vol. III. Madison: The University of Wisconsin Press, 1959.

Nietzsche, Friedrich. *Thus Spoke Zarathustra*, trans. Clancy Martin, with an introduction by Kathleen M. Higgins and Robert C. Solomon. New York: Barnes & Noble Classics, 2005.

Nihon no Shiika (*The Poetry of Japan*). Vol. 4: 'Tekkan Yosano, Akiko Yosano, Bokusui Wakayama and Isamu Yoshii'. Tokyo: Chuo Koron-sha Press, 1979.

Nippon Dai Hyakka Zensho (*Encyclopedia Nipponica*). Vol. 3. Tokyo: Shougaku-Kan Press, 1985.

Nishigaki, Osamu. 'Kansho Nooto' ('Note for Appreciation'). *Yosano Akiko Shiikashu* (*Selected Poems of Akiko Yosano*), ed. Jinbo Kotaro. Tokyo: Hakuo-sha Press, 1984. 181–92.

Noda, Utaro. 'Kaisetsu' ('Introduction'). *Midaregami* (*Tangled Hair*), ed. Utaro Noda. Kadokawa Library. Tokyo: Kadokawa-shoten, 1988. 116–37.

Norris, Margot. 'The Ontology of D. H. Lawrence's *St Mawr*'. *D. H. Lawrence: Modern Critical Views,* ed. Harold Bloom. New York. Chelsea House Publishers, 1986. 297–312.

Odagiri, Hideo. 'Jiyuu na Sei no Tegotae – Yosano Akiko toiu Sonzai' ('The Proof of Living Freely – the Existence of Akiko Yosano'). 'Gappo' ('monthly bulletin') no.1 of *Teihon Yosano Akiko Zenshu* (*The Collected Works of Akiko Yosano*). Vol. 1. Tokyo: Kodan-sha Press, 1979. 1–3.

Ohkuma, Akinobu. *D. H. Lawrence no Bungaku Jinruigakuteki Kousatsu – Seiai no Shinpishugi, Post-colonialism, Tandokusha wo Megutte* (*Literary Anthropological Investigations of D. H. Lawrence – On Mysticism in Sexual Love, Post-colonialism and Man's Central Aloneness*). Tokyo: Kazama Shobou Press, 2009.

Ohnuma, Tadahiro. *Jissen Qabalah: Jikotankyu no Tabi.* (*Practical Qabalah: a Journey for Self-Discovery*). Kyoto, Japan: Jinbun Shoin, 1988.

'Olga's Gallery' http://www.abcgallery.com/T/titian/titian (31 August 2003)

Panichas, George A. *Adventure in Consciousness: The Meaning of D. H. Lawrence's Religious Quest.* The Hague: Mouton, 1964.

Parrinder, Geoffrey. *Mysticism in the World's Religions.* London: Sheldon Press, 1976.

Peck, Harry Thurston, ed. *Harper's Dictionary of Classical Literature and Antiquities.* New York: Cooper Square Publishers, 1965.

Peers, Edgar A., trans. and ed. *The Complete Works of St. John of the Cross*, three volumes in one. Wheathampstead: Anthony Clarke, 1974.

Phillips, K. J. *Dying Gods in 20th-century Fiction.* Cranbury, NJ: Associated University Presses, 1990.

Poplawski, Paul. *The Works of D. H. Lawrence: A Chronological Checklist.* Nottingham: D. H. Lawrence Society, 1995.

Read, Herbert. 'Lawrence as a Painter'. *Paintings of D. H. Lawrence,* ed. Mervin Levy. London: Cory, Adams & Mackay, 1964. 55–64.

Ridler, A., ed. *Thomas Traherne: Poems, Centuries and Three Thanksgivings.* Oxford: Oxford University Press, 1966.

Rieff, Philip. 'The Therapeutic as Mythmaker'. *D. H. Lawrence: Modern Critical Views,* ed. Harold Bloom. New York. Chelsea House Publishers, 1986. 31–58.

Roberts, Warren, ed. *A Bibliography of D. H. Lawrence.* London: Rupert Hart-Davis, 1963.

Roberts, Warren, ed. *A Bibliography of D. H. Lawrence.* 2nd ed. Cambridge: Cambridge University Press, 1982.

Roberts, Warren, and Paul Poplawski, eds. *A Bibliography of D. H. Lawrence* 3rd ed. Cambridge: Cambridge University Press, 2001.

Sagar, Keith. *A Calendar of D. H. Lawrence.* Manchester: Manchester University Press, 1979.

Sagar, Keith. *D. H. Lawrence: Life into Art.* Harmondsworth: Penguin, 1985.

Sagar, Keith. 'Introduction'. *The Complete Short Novels of D. H. Lawrence,* ed. Keith Sagar and Melissa Partridge. Penguin English Library. Harmondsworth: Penguin, 1982. 26–45.

Sagar, Keith. *The Art of D. H. Lawrence.* Cambridge: Cambridge University Press, 1966.

Sagar, Keith. *The Life of D. H. Lawrence.* London: Eyre Methuen, 1980.

Sagar, Keith. 'Introduction'. *D. H. Lawrence's Paintings,* ed. Keith Sagar. London: Chaucer Press, 2003. 9–81.

Saito, Hiraku. 'Seikagaku, Seikyouiku: Kaisetu' ('Introduction to Sexology and Sexual Education'). *Sei to Seikyoiku no Jinkenmondai Shiryoshusei (Historical Documents of Human Rights Concerning Sex and Procreation).* Vol. 27. Tokyo: Fuji-shuppan, 2000. 1–8.

Salgado, Gamini N. 'The Poetry of D. H. Lawrence'. PhD dissertation. University of Nottingham. 1955. (unpublished)

Sargent, Helen Child and George Lyman Kittredge, eds. *English and Scottish Popular Ballads.* The Cambridge Edition. Boston: Houghton Mifflin, 1904.

Sato, Akio. *Midaregami ko (A Study of Tangled Hair). Kindaisakka Kenkyu Sosho (A Series of Studies on Modern Japanese Authors)* No. 104. Tokyo: Nihontosho Centre, 1990; reprint of the 1956 edition published by Shudo-sha Press, Tokyo.

Sato, Haruo. *Akiko Mandala.* Kodansha Bugei Library. Tokyo: Kodan-sha Press, 1993.

Sato, Haruo. 'Kaisetsu' ('Introduction'). *Yasano Akiko Kashu (Selected Tanka Poems of Akiko Yosano),* ed. Sato Haruo. Shincho Library. Tokyo: Shincho-sha Press, 1953. 190–208.

Shapard, Leslie, ed. *Encyclopedia of Occultism and Parapsychology.* Vol. II. Detriot: Gale Research Co., 1979.

Shincho Nihon Bungaku Jiten (The Shincho Dictionary of Japanese Literature). Tokyo: Shincho-sha Press, 1988.

Simpson, Jacqueline and Steve Roud, eds. *A Dictionary of English Folklore.* Oxford: Oxford University Press, 2000.

Smith, Margaret. *An Introduction to Mysticism.* New York: Oxford University Press, 1977.

Spilka, Mark. *The Love Ethic of D. H Lawrence.* Bloomington: Indiana University Press, 1955.

Squires, Michael. *The Pastoral Novel: Studies in George Eliot, Thomas Hardy, and D. H. Lawrence.* Charlottesville: University Press of Virginia, 1974.

Starvou, Constatine Nicholas. *William Blake and D. H. Lawrence: A Comparative Study in the Similarity of their Thought.* PhD dissertation. University of Buffalo, 1952. Ann Arbor: UMI Dissertation Information Service, 1987.

Suzuki, Shunji. 'D. H. Lawrence no Umi – Shoki to Kouki no Shi ni Saguru' ('The Sea in D. H. Lawrence – A Study of his Early and Later Poems'). *Studies in English Literature* (Tokyo: Literary Society of Japan) 55 (2) (December, 1978). 261–76.

Taiyo (*The Sun*). Vol.1 No.8 (1895), 146–54 (Kunitake Kume, 'Rinri no Kairyo' ('The Improvement of Ethics')); Vol.2 No.22 (1896), 94–5 (Yoshiharu Iwamoto, 'Jiyu Kekkon no Shui' ('The Main Point of Free Marriage')); Vol. 5 No. 5 (1899), 173–6 (Namiko Sassa, 'Danjo Kousai no Koto' (1) ('On Communications between Man and Woman')); Vol.5 No.6 (1899), 159–61 (Namiko Sassa, 'Danjo Kousai no Koto' (2) ('On Communications between Man and Woman')).

Takeda, Izumo. 'Ashiyadouman Oouchikagami Kuzunoha' ('The Fox-Wife in the Forest of Shinoda'). *Haktaza Ookabuki June 1999.* Fukuoka: Hakata Theatre, 1999. 5–9.

Taylor, Stephen. 'Lawrence the Mystic'. *The Journal of the D. H Lawrence Society 2001.* 62–74.

Teikokubungaku (*Literature of the Empire*). Vol.1, No.11(1895), 100–01 'Zappou' ('Miscellanea'); Vol.2, No. 5 (1896), 102 'Zappou' ('Miscellanea'); Vol.3, No.8 (1897), 52–62 (Gyoro Hayakawa, 'Bungei niokeru Josei' ('Women in Literature')); Vol.5, No.6 (1899), 101 (Kuriputomeria, 'Kinseino Joseibikan' ('The Modern View of Women's Beauty')).

Thoreau, Henry David. *Walden and Other Writings of Henry David Thoreau,* ed. Brooks Atkinson. The Modern Library. New York: Random House, 1950.

Ukiyoe Taikei (*Ukiyoe Series*). Vols. 13, 16 and 17. Tokyo: Shuei-sha Press, 1976.

Vickery, John B. *The Literary Impact of* The Golden Bough. Princeton: Princeton University Press, 1973.

Viinikka, Anja. *From Persephone to Pan: D. H. Lawrence's Mythopoeic Vision of the Integrated Personality with Special Emphasis on the Short Fiction and Other Writings in the Early Nineteen Twenties.* Turku, Finland: Turun Yliopitso, 1988.

Vivas, Eliseo. *D. H. Lawrence: The Failure and the Triumph of Art.* Evanston: Northwestern University Press, 1960.

Wilde, Alan. 'The Illusion of *St. Mawr*: Technique and Vision in D. H. Lawrence's Novel'. *D. H. Lawrence: Critical Assessments.* Vol. III., ed. David Ellis and Ornella De Zordo. Mountfield: Helm Information, 1992. 324–35.

Worthen, John. *D. H. Lawrence and the Idea of the Novel.* London: Macmillan, 1979.

Wright, Terry R. *D. H. Lawrence and the Bible.* Cambridge: Cambridge University Press, 2000.

Yosano, Akiko. 'Fujin no Darakusuru Saidaigen'in' (The Greatest Cause of Women's Depravation'). *Teihon Yasano Akiko Zenshu* (*The Collected Works of Akiko Yosano*). Vol.15. Tokyo: Kodan-sha Press, 1979. 289–96.

Yosano, Akiko. 'Hirakibumi' ('The Opened Letter'). *Yosano Akiko Hyoronshu* (*Critical Essays of Akiko Yosano*), ed. Masanao Kano and Nobuko Kouuchi. Iwanami Library. Tokyo: Iwanami-shoten, 1985. 16–23.

Yosano, Akiko. 'Hiratsuka, Yamakawa, Yamada Sanjoshi ni Kotau' ('My Reply to Mrss. Hiratsuka, Yamakawa, and Yamada'). *Yosano Akiko Hyoronshu* (*Critical Essays of Akiko Yosano*), ed. Masanao Kano and Nobuko Kouuchi. Iwanami Library. Tokyo: Iwanami-shoten, 1985. 219–36.

Yosano, Akiko. 'Hiratsukasan to Watashi no Ronso' ('My Skirmish with Mrs. Hiratsuka'). *Yosano Akiko Hyoronshu* (*Critical Essays of Akiko Yosano*), ed. Masanao Kano and Nobuko Kouuchi. Iwanami Library. Tokyo: Iwanami-shoten, 1985. 200–10.

Yosano, Akiko. *Midaregami* (*Tangled Hair*), ed. Utaro Noda. Kadokawa Library. Tokyo: Kadokawa-shoten, 1988.

Yosano, Akiko. *Midaregami: Chocolate-Word Translation,* trans. Machi Tawara. Tokyo: Kawadeshobo-shinsha, 1998.

Yosano, Akiko. 'Rodan Ou ni Atta Hi' ('The Day When I Met Old Rodin'). *Teihon Yasano Akiko Zenshu* (*The Collected Works of Akiko Yosano*). Vol.15. Tokyo: Kodan-sha Press, 1979. 336–42.

Yosano, Akiko. 'Sei no Kyoiku' ('Education of Sex'). *Teihon Yasano Akiko Zenshu* (*The Collected Works of Akiko Yosano*). Vol. 18. Tokyo: Kodan-sha Press, 1979. 412–14

Yosano, Akiko. *Tangled Hair: Selected Tanka from 'Midaregami'*, trans. Sanford Goldstein and Seishi Shinoda. Tokyo: Charles E. Tuttle, 1987.

Yosano, Akiko. *Yasano Akiko Kashu* (*Selected Tanka Poems of Akiko Yosano*), ed. Haruo Sato. Shincho Library. Tokyo: Shincho-sha Press, 1953.

Yosano, Akiko. *Yosano Akiko Hyoronshu* (*Critical Essays of Akiko Yosano*), ed. Masanao Kono and Kouuchi Nobuko. Iwanami Library. Tokyo: Iwanami-shoten, 1985.

Yosano, Akiko. *Yosano Akiko Shiika Shu* (*Selected Poems of Akiko Yosano*), ed. Kotaro Jinbo. Tokyo: Hakuho-sha Press, 1984.

INDEX